EDITED BY JAMES LANGFORD & LEROY S. ROUNER

WALKING
WITH
GOD
IN A
FRAGILE
WORLD

WALKING WITH GOD IN A FRAGILE WORLD

Published by
CORBY BOOKS
A Division of Corby Publishing, LP
P.O. Box 93
Notre Dame, IN 46556
11961 Tyler Road
Lakeville, IN 46536
(574) 784-3482

WALKING WITH GOD IN A FRAGILE WORLD

EDITED BY
JAMES LANGFORD & LEROY S. ROUNER

CONTENTS

Introduction v

Part One
PATHS AND PASSAGES

Part Two
BELIEVING IS SEEING

Part Three

PAST THE GATES OF HELL

INTRODUCTION
to the Paperback Edition

The origins of this book followed upon the horrors of 9/11. My colleague and close friend Leroy Rouner and I were trying to decipher what that event said about the state of the world, the balance between good and evil, our own contingency in the face of the fragility of life, and the crucial question: Where was God in all of this? We decided to invite some of the best spiritual writers of our time to contribute original reflections, representing Christian, Jewish and Muslim perspectives, and to build a book that would power genuine soul searching by our readers.

In some ways we succeeded. Our roster of authors is stellar, and the essays present a variety of approaches—each explores, without assertion, the questions so needing attention and meditation in our time. These essays have no time limitations; the issues beg for understanding, or at least exploration, today as much as they did on the day after 9/11. We wish only that more people had found the book and used it as a launching pad for their own meditations. We hope that providing the book in a paperback format will stimulate a wider audience to think about these things and seek a walk with God to discuss them.

The challenges raised so drastically on September 11 keep coming back in one form or another—Columbine, Aurora, Ft. Hood, hurricanes Sandy and Katrina, Newtown, Boston, and Moore, Oklahoma—stare us in the face and cry out for answers. We might wonder how, when confronted by the litany of death and destruction, could there really be an all-loving, all-powerful God? We tell ourselves yes, there is, but not the one we thought we knew, not the God we pray to for protection and life. There are easy answers, of course, but often they ring hollow and yield the possibility that we have done God the disservice of picturing God as a magician, a dictator, a scorekeeper or a Santa Claus to whom we can appeal with a gift list detailing what we want. We hear it said at funerals that God needed him or her even more than we did and so God took the deceased from our midst. But God doesn't kill people—nature does, people do, age does, disease does. Perhaps we need to re-define what we think God does and doesn't author and direct. I will die not because God wants me to or "needs" me. I will die because something—accident, age, illness or violence—will rob my body of its ability to host my soul. If that is true, we need to be praying for the grace to live well and die with courage.

Every day we have to live with uncertainty as to the day or the hour. We can live with hope even as we face life's fragility and our own contingency. I don't think God wants or needs us to suffer hunger, poverty, loneliness, discrimination or disease. Perhaps what God wants is for us to care for each other, nurture each other and work together to grow the economy of love in the world. God is love. As the song says, "Love is all you need."

To be anthropomorphic about it, if God cried, God's tears would drown the world. And if God smiled, we would not need the stars. But God does neither. Creation is God's mosaic and it cannot be completed until evil is vanquished by an abundance of good. In that sense, God does need us to add to the sum of goodness in the world. Sometimes this seems hopeless, surely a long shot. But if we help each other, if we walk with God, if we find and encourage the goodness in others, if we learn to serve, then we can cry for Him and smile for Him. We are His hands, His eyes, His heart on earth. The authors of these essays all see with the eyes of their faith. Instead of "seeing is believing," they reflect the conviction that "believing is seeing." The reality they see is God acting in the world through grace and inspiration. It is our hope that you, the reader, will see the same.

– James Langford

This edition is dedicated to the memory of
Leroy Rouner, William Sloane Coffin, Peter J. Gomes and Sue Shidler

Part One

PATHS AND PASSAGES

"Now—here is my secret: I tell it to you with an openness of heart that I doubt I shall ever achieve again, so I pray you are in a quiet room as you hear these words. My secret is that I need God—that I am sick and can no longer make it alone. I need God to help me give, because I no longer seem capable of giving; to help me be kind, as I no longer seem capable of kindness; to help me love, as I seem beyond being able to love."

—Douglas Coupland, *Life after God*

I
WALKING IN THE WORLD
WITH A FRAGILE GOD
FREDERICK BUECHNER

There is no doubt that the world is fragile. For whatever the reason, God seems to have made it that way. It is true that God divided the primordial waters of chaos into two parts, creating the firmament of heaven to keep the world safe from the waters above and the waters below by confining them to one place called the sea, but it is not only the story of Noah and the flood that attests to the hard fact that the system is by no means foolproof. By placing the fatal tree of the knowledge of good and evil in the center of the garden, God saw to it that not even Eden was to be a warm nest, and by giving human beings from that day forward the same freedom to choose between being children of God or problem children, God ensured that all human history would be equally at peril. The return of chaos is a perpetual possibility. There is always another holocaust getting ready to blaze up. There is always another Ivan the Terrible or Idi Amin or Saddam Hussein waiting in the wings. The missiles are always in their silos needing only the push of the wrong finger on the right button to unleash the unthinkable.

When all hell broke loose on September 11, I was lying in bed in Brigham and Womens Hospital in Boston, Massachusetts, where five days earlier I had undergone total hip replacement surgery. I couldn't walk at all, with God or without God. I couldn't so much as roll over in bed without help. The morning the news broke, the tall, young New Zealand orthopedist who had operated on me came into the room to ask how I was doing, and after telling him, I asked the same question of him. Not so good, he said. A couple he and his family knew had been on one of the two planes on their way from Boston to Los Angeles to see a new grandchild for the first time. He had had to tell his children about it at breakfast, and they had taken it badly. As soon as he left, I covered my face with my hands and wept, not like a child as I was about to say, but like a seventy-five-year-old man who felt as helpless as a child— not just to walk but to know what to say, what to think, what to do, what to be.

Much of the rest of the day I lay there on my back watching the endless TV replays of the unspeakably beautiful September morning with the plane, golden in the early sun, aimed like an arrow at the second tower. I have always known the world is fragile and life is fragile and my own small life more fragile still as it enters its last chapter, but like most of us I had never really known before that for all its purple mountains' majesty and fruited plains with God's grace shed upon them as golden as the September sun, America the heartbreakingly, heartbrokenly beautiful, is fragile too. If the events of September 11 could happen here, I suddenly realized, then anything could happen anytime and anywhere. There was no place on the planet to escape Terror.

After a few days I reached the point where I could walk a few halting steps all bent over an aluminum walker, but I don't remember any thought of God's somehow walking with me. In fact I don't remember thinking much about God at all. God seemed remote and ectoplasmic compared to the devastation that had taken place in New York. I believe I thought mostly about my grandchildren, the then eight small boys and one small girl who are the bright stars of my old age, and about what lay ahead for them in a future I would not live to see. Anthrax was the next thing that filled the TV screen. Germ warfare. Osama bin Laden looking not unlike pictures of Jesus in his white robe and beard likely to strike again at any moment. It was mostly about the nine small children that the terrorists had terrorized me.

I suppose I must have prayed for God to protect them, but I knew in my heart that that has never been God's style. I suppose it is because if God were to start stepping in to protect people, where would the process stop? If God steps in to protect us every time all hell is about to break loose, if only for one of us at a time, then what becomes of our human freedom to go it on our own instead of being merely like puppets in a puppet show? And if human beings are not free, how can they be truly human? If human beings are created above all else to love one another freely and to love God freely, how can they not also be free not to love one another at all but to do appalling things to each other instead like blowing up a man and his wife on their way to see a new grandchild, like replacing a God of justice and mercy with a God who sanctifies the decimation of thousands of innocents. Maybe the world's terrible fragility is the price God is willing to pay for humankind's holy and terrible freedom to be sinners or saints or the kind of hybrids that most of us are most of the time.

I don't remember thinking about God much at all during those long days in that hospital room. I had brought a Bible with me, but it was hard to read with its tiny print, and I didn't feel much like reading it anyway; it not only didn't bring me comfort but somehow depressed me, summoning up not so much the mystery of the Holy as what is so often the unholy tedium of church. A Roman Catholic chaplain came to see me one day, and I liked him. He asked me if I wanted him to pray for me, and after he did, I asked him if I could pray for him. So we became something like friends for as long as I was there, and he would stick his head in the door every once in a while when he was passing by. I'm sure I said prayers at other times too, but I don't remember anything in particular about them. I don't remember any strong sense that God was paying much attention to them, or even that I was. But during those days when I was trying to walk again, if God was not with me in any of the traditional places where God is supposed to be, or in any of the traditional ways, I can believe now that God was with me even so, although it wasn't until later that I began to realize it fully.

As is apt to happen with susceptible male patients, I fell in love with one of my nurses. She was a young woman from the Aran Islands named Susie. She was not married, but she had a brother who was visiting from Ireland, and I twitted her about taking time off to be with him every now and again when it was clearly her duty, I said, to stay and take care of me instead. She was slender and graceful with a face full of fun and freshness, and one day when she was performing for me a particularly squalid nursely task, I asked her why on earth a lovely young woman like her had ever taken on a job that involved so much that was unpleasant and demeaning.

Her answer didn't sound like something she had learned in nursing school but like something that had come straight out of the truth of who she was, and it caught me completely off guard. She said she didn't think of it as unpleasant and demeaning to clean people up after they had used the bedpan. She said as a nurse she was there to help people feel better and get better and that was just one of the ways she tried to do it.

That was the first time I had an inkling of what was going on in that hospital, and when I reached the point of using crutches with Susie following close behind to catch me if I started to fall, I glimpsed again what she had become for me during those trying and terrorizing days, began to glimpse who it was I was walking with. Nor was she the only one.

The two disciples on their way to Emmaus recognized Jesus in the breaking of the bread, and looking back I think I can recognize him not just in Susie from the Aran Islands but in virtually every nurse and every doctor I had, not to mention all the others who came in to mop the floor or bring my tray or draw my blood. In more ways than just literally, I'm not sure I would ever really have walked again without them.

Without him.

WALKING IN THE WORLD WITH A FRAGILE GOD

Before being admitted to the hospital I was told that patients were advised not to bring with them any pieces of jewelry or other items of value, and I complied by leaving at home two things. One of them was a signet ring I wear engraved with the Latin words that C. G. Jung had carved into the stone above the door to his house in Switzerland— *vocatus atque non vocatus Deus aderit,* which in translation is "summoned or not summoned God will be present." The other thing was a small gold cross that I wear around my neck under my shirt.

When I got home, the ring, as I slipped it back on my finger, confirmed what I had learned yet again in the hospital. I hadn't done much of anything in the way of summoning God there or of even paying much attention to God, but God had been present anyway, and present *there* of all places where I felt paralyzed by my total helplessness as well as by the terrorized helplessness of the fragile world in which it felt as though even God was paralyzed. The word "hospital" is related both to the word "host" and to the word "guest," and through Susie and the others, God's role had been that of the host, who, without waiting to be asked, offers refreshment, healing, and hope to the guests, like me, who are strangers and yet not strangers at all. And in the person of the Roman Catholic chaplain and the others, both friends and family, who came to see me, he was of course also the guest.

But the cross when I slipped it back over my head, getting my wife to close the little clasp which I had never been able to do for myself, spoke to me what seemed a significantly different kind of word. It is not just the world we walk in that is fragile, it seemed to say, but God also is fragile. It is not just the world that is vulnerable to the worst that mankind can do, but God also is vulnerable. The Twin Towers had been reduced to a smoldering mountain of rubble with who knows how many thousands of victims buried in it dead, dying, or alive, and what the cross under my shirt seemed to be saying was that one of the victims was God.

When someone we love suffers, we also suffer—that is what love is all about—but if we could somehow wish our suffering away, I think we would choose not to because the suffering and the loving are so inextricably bound up in each other that to wish one away would be to wish the other away as well. And could that be true, I wondered, also of God? To speak of God suffering is to be guilty of the heresy of patripassionism, but, at the risk of hellfire, I tend to hold to it anyway. When I covered my face with my hands and wept at the surgeon's account of his friends on the second plane, I cannot for a moment but believe that in one way or another God was not also weeping with me.

In good Protestant fashion, my small gold cross is an empty one suggesting that when Jesus rose from the dead and ascended to God's right hand, his passion ended once and for all. He doesn't suffer anymore, and because, as Christians are called to be his body, to use the most haunting of St. Paul's images, now that he has been caught up in the place that passes all understanding, maybe we are called to suffer for the world in his place. Who can say? But if that is indeed part of the truth of the empty cross, there is also the truth of the cross with the body in torment still on it—the truth that as long as there is so much as one child crying at breakfast, as long as there is just one old man crying into his hands, then Jesus cries too because the God who is in him is also crying. Jesus is fragile with God's fragility.

The gospel story can be read as the story of a man to whom, in his fragility, almost every bad thing happens that can happen, a man not unlike the tragic-comic figure of the little tramp in the old Chaplin comedies. Jesus is born not in the shelter of home with a whole family to welcome him but in the stable of an inn that has no room for him and among the beasts who couldn't care less whether he is born or not. As an infant he barely escapes death at the hands of a paranoid tyrant. He spends his life on the road proclaiming a truth that the ones he is closest to, including his own mother, dismiss as aberrational. He tells marvelous stories and performs marvelous deeds that seem to have left most of the people who witnessed them cold as far as any lasting effect that they may have had on them. He was written off by the Jews as a blasphemer, and, as a threat to the peace, he was condemned by the Romans to a death so hideous that, when he saw it coming, he begged the God he called father not to let it happen. Yet, he received not so much as a whisper in reply so that he "sweated blood," as the Gospels put it, and, not long afterward, died in agony crying out that even God had abandoned him.

Crosses that, unlike the one I put back on when I returned home on my crutches, still bear the body of the crucified on them testify to the truth that Jesus is eternally vulnerable to the mockery, brutality, and indifference of humankind. Part of the world's fragility is that the God we are called to walk with is no less fragile than the world is, than we are, perhaps because God no more chooses to be invulnerable to suffering than Jesus chose to call down legions of angels to save him from the suffering of the cross. Perhaps the God who is revealed in Jesus chooses fragility instead because to be free to suffer when the beloved suffers is at the very heart of what loving is. Perhaps the veiling of the cross on Good Friday is a way of signifying that, like us, God covers God's face with God's hands when the pain is too much even for God to bear any other way.

Nothing could be cloudier or more futile than such speculations as these, but one thing that seems beyond all doubt is that, if not God, then the whole business of believing in God in our time is as fragile as glass. Those who commend it most loudly and famously are apt to be for the most part charlatans, simpletons, and right-wing polemicists, whereas many of the others seem to be little more than *professional* believers who pronounce banalities, pieties, and truisms with the relentless energy of insurance salesmen. The Catholic Church is in a turmoil over the sexual felonies of its priesthood together with the attempts to cover them up by its bishops and cardinals and even, it would appear, with the knowledge if not the connivance of the pope. Tapes have been released of Billy Graham swapping anti-Semitisms with Richard Nixon. And far less sensationally, but in the long run even more devastatingly, what goes on in far too many churches all over the land is often so shallow, so passionless, so theologically doctrinaire, unimaginative, and unconvincing that it is not hard to imagine the day when, as has already happened all over England, church buildings will have been converted to gift shops and restaurants for the tourist trade or left for their roofs to fall in and their stained glass to shatter and turn to dust.

Maybe that is the best thing that can happen. Churches die, but God does not die. God will never be without witnesses. And if the church as we know it goes under at last as it may well deserve to do, there will still be left both our fragile God and each other in all our fragility. And that is where it all started in the first place. That is at the heart of what the true and invisible church is all about, and of what walking with God is all about, and not even all of the forces of international terrorism will be able to prevail against the fragile loveliness of that September morning with hardly a cloud in the sky.

II

GOD AND THE WORLD'S DISORDERS
WILLIAM SLOANE COFFIN

How is it possible to believe in a loving God, knowing as we do that almost every square inch of the earth's surface is soaked with the tears and blood of the innocents? Either a good God is not altogether powerful or a powerful God is not altogether good. On this matter of obvious concern to every serious believer, I would like to offer a few personal thoughts.

Human life has always been precarious but in recent times the world itself has become fragile. Decades ago Albert Camus wrote: "Probably every generation sees itself as charged with remaking the world. Mine, however, knows that its task will not be merely to remake the world. Its task is even greater; to keep the world from destroying itself."

Then in the 1980s at the height of the Cold War, a group of neutral nations, trying in vain to curb the Soviet-American nuclear arms race, warned ominously: "The world has become as a prisoner in a cell, condemned to death, awaiting the uncertain moment of execution." To be more precise, it is not really the world but the human race that is fragile, and getting ever more so as it is far from certain that we care enough for future generations to pay the price for their survival.

About my own religious quest, I want to begin over fifty years ago. Four years in the army during World War II exposed me to far too much cruelty for my boyhood innocence to survive. As an infantry officer in Europe and, for two years, a liaison officer with the Soviet army, I came to realize that the stream of human life was sullied and bloody. And as if Nazism and fascism weren't savage enough, the Soviet Union clearly was to marxism as the Ku Klux Klan has been to Christianity. So upon entering college in the fall of 1947, my primary purpose was to study the human condition.

I suppose I could have studied Freud and Jung, but, at the time, those who spoke most directly to me were, on the one hand, the atheistic French existentialists, particularly Camus, Sartre, and Malraux, and on the other hand, the American theologians Richard Niebuhr, Reinhold Niebuhr, and Paul Tillich. I was an eager student soon to become all too aware of how right Tolstoy was when he suggested that certain questions are put to human beings not so much to get an answer to them as to spend a lifetime wrestling with them. I continued to doubt the existence of God, but, I think, out of a passionate love of the truth, not out of a pathological need to doubt.

As regards Christianity, two things put me off. First, the churches just then were beginning to desert the city in droves, fleeing to the suburbs following their middle-class constituents. Second, I was turned off by the decidedly ungenerous orthodoxy of some fundamentalist students anxious to speed my conversion to their understanding of Christianity. Their answers seemed too pat, their submissions to God too ready. It seemed to me that too easy submission was but a façade for repressed rebellion. I suspected that, deep down, many of these students were hostile.

But attracted though I was intellectually to Sartre, and especially to Camus, I held back. They were asking the right questions, and their despair was real, but I couldn't help thinking the way they met suffering was a bit romantic, even a bit arrogant. It was as if they were boasting that non-believers suffered more than do the faithful, which struck me as a truly pointless form of competition. By contrast, the theologians seemed to be in touch with a deeper reality if only I too could find it. Like the existentialists, they knew what hell was all about, but in the depths of it they found a heaven, which made more sense out of everything, much as light gives meaning to darkness.

Most helpful were Bach's *St. John Passion* and *St. Matthew Passion*, and the requiems of Brahms, Verdi, and Faure. Prior to World War II, I had aspired to be a concert pianist and so I had no trouble in realizing that religious truths, like those of music, art, and poetry, are, on a deeper level, more apprehended than comprehended; they are truths that the mind can correct but not discover. Therefore, the so-called leap of faith seemed to me less a leap of thought than of action. Faith was impossible without trust. While such insights were hardly enough to convert me, they encouraged me to accept the wise advice of Alcoholics Anonymous: "I will commit as much of myself as I can to as much of God as I believe in." Drawn to seminary upon graduation from college, I found the commitment growing continuously through three more wonderful years of education. In the meantime, the world appeared bent on more and more madness.

I understand those who want to hold God responsible for the world's disorders. But consider for a moment an imaginative Mormon myth. At Creation's start Christ and Satan were each requested to submit to God a plan for dealing with the infant human race that already was showing signs of delinquency. Satan's plan was simple (the kind that secretaries of defense frequently come up with): God has armies of angels at his command; why not assign an angel with punitive power to each human being? That should keep the race in line, and things moving along nicely.

In other words, Satan was the first "hard-liner," urging upon God the virtues of force. And isn't that what most of us do? When thing go badly for us personally—or nationally—don't we expect God, rather than ourselves, to straighten out the mess? Shouldn't God, at the very least, keep our children safe and sound, no matter how fast they drive? And shouldn't God keep the human race from annihilating itself, no matter what fiendish weapons we invent and insist on deploying? If ultimately children and the human race are to be saved only by force, then so be it, by force—"But save us, God."

In contrast to Satan's, Christ's plan was crazy but brilliant, implying a regard for humanity so high that Satan must have mocked it. "Let them have free will and go their own way," Christ proposed to God, "only let me live and die as one of them, both as an example of how to live, and to show them how much you care for them."

Following this myth to its conclusion, we can say that Christmas makes it clear what plan God chose to implement. And Christmas makes it equally clear that love is always self-restricting when it comes to power. Parents can understand that; we finally can't protect, only support our children. So it is with God. God provides maximum support, minimal protection. The parable of the Prodigal Son is really about the prodigal love of the father, a father who by refusing to give him his share of the inheritance, could have kept his wayward son at home. But he could not have kept him filial. So he releases him into the storms of the world and waits on the road until he sees him "afar off."

If, as Scripture says, "God is love," then human freedom is for real. As Dostoyevsky's Grand Inquisitor properly discerned, freedom is a burden, choice is scary. But freedom is the absolutely necessary precondition of love. We are not slaves but children of our Father, free to do good, free to sin.

So, when in anguish over any human violence done to innocent victims, we ask of God: "How could you let that happen?" it is well to remember that God at that very moment is asking the exact same question of us.

God doesn't go around the world with fingers on triggers, his fist around knives, and his hands on the controls of airplanes. It's outrageous to credit God with the worst follies of humankind. They're our fault—and they break a loving God's heart. We're to blame for desecrating God's creation, ravaging the earth as if there were no tomorrow. It's our fault—and shame—that we show so little imaginative sympathy for the plight of the poor. And God who beats "swords into plowshares and spears into pruning hooks" surely must long to have us ponder Thomas Mann's contention that "war is a coward's escape from the problems of peace."

The essential reality of human existence is ethical. The world swings on an ethical hinge; mess with that hinge and both nature and history will feel the shock. It's all up to us. God will not intervene at the expense of human freedom. But ask of God a thimbleful of help to cope with the treachery and disappointments of life and you will get an oceanful in return. Once again, God provides maximum support, minimum protection. In short, we are called on to respond not to God's power but rather to God's love. With Dietrich Bonhoeffer I believe we are helped more by God's weakness than by God's strength. Both the Christmas manger and the Good Friday cross are symbols of God's weakness. Understandably we want God to be strong—so that we can be weak. But God wants to be weak so that we can be strong. Maybe God had to come to earth as a child so that we who are adults might finally grow up to assume the moral responsibilities our freedom entails.

Clearly all human beings have more in common than

they have in conflict, and it is precisely when what they have in conflict is about to tear the world apart that what they have in common needs most to be affirmed. What does this say to the sundry religions of the world that have so much in common—besides their many falls from grace which have hobbled and disfigured the religious quest throughout history?

In a recent and unusually fine interview, President Joseph Hough of Union Theological Seminary in New York took up the question of "religious toleration." While desirable, Hough insists, it is "not sufficient in a world of religious pluralism." He notes that even the most influential Christian theologians during the twentieth century "failed to see the limitations of toleration." They have conceded only that other faiths may be "lesser lights" (Karl Barth), or that representatives of other faiths may be saved because they are "Christians incognito" (Paul Tillich), or "anonymous Christians" (Karl Rahner). Tolerance like this concedes only "minimal value to other religious traditions."

I am grateful to President Hough for his clear stand on this matter, for if our imperiled planet is to survive, religious folk of diverse faiths must seriously seek to overcome their shameful divisions and together do all in their power to heal the wounds of our fractured world.

Years ago in seminary, troubled by the exclusiveness of the church toward Muslims, I remembered vividly the day it dawned on me that the divinity of Christ meant not so much that Christ was like God as that God was like Christ. In other words, when Christians see Christ healing the hurt, empowering the weak, scorning the powerful, they are seeing transparently the power of God at work. In theological terms, Christocentric means Theocentric. To believe, as do Christians, that God is best defined by Christ is not to say that God is confined to Christ. As Hough says, "What is essential for Christian faith is that we know we have seen the face of God in the face of Jesus Christ. It is not essential to believe that no one else has seen God and experienced redemption in another time and place."

All religions are different—that's certain. But most religions seek to fulfill the same function, that is, they strive to convert people from self-preoccupation to the whole-hearted giving up of oneself in love for God and for others. Therefore it makes sense for religious people to move from truth-claiming to the function truth plays. "By their fruits you shall know them," means that the way we believe is as important as what we believe; it's the way we do things as well as the things we do.

I said the essence of human reality is ethical. St. Paul says, "Make love your aim." Jews, Muslims, and a host of other believers would agree. Listen to Rabbi Abraham Joshua Heschel: "A religious person is a person who holds God and humanity in one thought at one time, at all times, who suffers harm done to other, whose greatest passion is compassion, whose greatest strength is love and defiance of despair."

It is a bedrock conviction of many religious faiths that all six billion of us on the planet belong one to another. That's the way God made us. From a Christian point of view, Christ died to keep us that way. Our sin is only and always that we put asunder what God has joined together.

I believe good religion makes justice and mercy, that is, love, the central value of human life. It is bad religion to deify doctrines and creeds. While creeds and doctrines are indispensable to religious life, they are also only signposts. Love is the sole hitching post. The reasons are clear: doctrines can divide, doctrines also are not immune to error. Let's not forget the many doctrines that once upheld slavery and apartheid, and the few that still keep women in the status of second-class citizens. But while doctrines can divide love can only unite.

Much the same can be said of religious traditions. Never should we ignore the wisdom of our ancestors. But a tradition is not an oracle; rather, it is a constant challenge, an unending task. And a tradition that cannot be changed also cannot be preserved. That lesson is as old as history itself.

Put differently, religious people have always both to recover tradition and to recover from it.

In our tormented and endangered world, few things, I imagine, could be more pleasing to God than for people of all faiths to join together in pledging allegiance "to the earth and to the flora and fauna and human life that it supports; one planet indivisible with clean air, soil, and water, with liberty, and justice and peace for all."

But to implement that allegiance will take all the power of perseverance that religious faith affords. Change comes hard. Spiritual maturity takes a long time. Amaziah the priest was right to say of Amos the prophet, "The land cannot bear his words." Centuries later, echoing the same thought, Elizabeth Janeway wrote: "There's nothing more ubiquitously pervasive than an idea whose time won't go."

If you believe, as many believers do, in a politically engaged spirituality and you're trying to save the environment; if you are persuaded that economic crimes can cause damage as extensive as the crimes of violence so endemic in the world today; and if you're an American trying to temper patriotic fervor with a healthy dose of national humility, you're bound at times to feel like quitting. But if Jesus never allowed his soul to be cornered into despair, and if it was to those farthest from the seats of power that he said, "You are the salt of the earth . . . you are the light of the world"—who then are we to quit "fighting the good fight of faith"?

With poet Grace Paley, we see today "a widening darkness between our lucky stars." Clearly the planet will not forever endure our insults. It's time for moral outrage.

At the same time we must pray for grace to contend against wrong without becoming wrongly contentious, grace to fight pretensions of national righteousness without personal self-righteousness. Such grace comes largely through those who will laugh and weep with us, those who will picket and pray with us, and those who will never let us forget the wonders and beauty of God's creation.

III
UNLESS YOU BECOME LIKE CHILDREN
JAMES LANGFORD

I live my life with a mind trained to be sensitive to theological insights, and the memory of moments when I really did sense that I was walking with God in a world that only seemed to be fragile. In seven years of seminary training, the worldview I adopted was compact, all-embracing, and certain. Goodness was everywhere, first caused by a loving God. Evil, the lack of being and of good, was permitted, not willed by God: essentially negative, not positive. I wanted to sense God's presence, to see Christ in others, to overcome anything that threatened to hinder my desire to please God. In the confines of a monastic setting, my days were ordered and tranquil, my beliefs were real and wonderfully coherent Those were good days. I will never look back and call them naive or curse them as a waste of mind and life.

The point is that it all had meaning then. I loved the values of my belief, the certainty of my encompassing worldview. Loneliness was there, but time and a closer relationship to God would, I hoped, one day purge it. Friendship was there, but always contained by the warnings of time-honored asceticism. I could pray then, but most often in ritual manner or by offering up some sacrifice or humiliation. I saw suffering—my own and others'—not as needing alleviation so much as Job-like endurance. I felt ready to be a prophet, but with a mission more like Isaiah's than Ezekial's: to challenge rather than to console.

But when I left that world and sought dispensation from the commitments it required, it seemed to me that the

God I had tried to walk with went into hiding. Or, perhaps more accurately, like Adam, it was I who was hiding and if God was calling out to me, His voice was so faint that I could claim not to hear it as I now explored a world for which I was not prepared. It was like coming out of suspended animation: there I was, walking the streets of New York City searching for a job, discovering that my neat and compact universe seemed like some utopian dream, surely not able to survive the struggling, grasping, grueling nature of life in the secular city. I had left my shelter, left those moments when God seemed so real and so radiant, and gone into the world to see for myself what Nietzsche and Sartre, Camus and Tillich had seen and tried to comprehend.

It was hard to hear God now that His voice was not being played back to me. Instead, I heard the pent-up frustrations unleashed by the militants of the late 1960s, the political speeches full of promises never to be kept, and a nationalism that urged every citizen to subscribe to a myth symbolized by destroying a village to save its inhabitants from communism. Where would I hear God? On a subway jammed with people who, for the moment, have to forget their humanity? In the constant pressure to budget in order to pay for the essentials of life? What does the doctrine of evil as the "privation of good that should be present" have to say to the multitudes who suffer from poverty, powerlessness, loneliness, and abuse? How can one find Christ in others when, all too often, his disguise is so varied and so complete? How are we supposed to lose ourselves until we find ourselves, to become like Christ until we have become ourselves? How can we mean prayers that plead for mercy to a majestic God who is perfectly, unchangeably happy, and therefore logically unmoved by our plight or our plea? Somehow, perhaps we need to believe that God, figuratively at least, breathes smog as we do, that He is not the Great Strategic Planner/Manipulator, but rather someone who sees the need once in a while to change course. Perhaps God cannot simply sponsor the program, He must be in it as well.

I wrote at the time: "Having left the shelter of my certitudes, I need to find a personal spirituality that can live and grow in the midst of chaos and apparent absurdity. I have begun to embrace uncertainty, to live with process, with risk. To live, I mean really live in the active sense, is to risk, to recognize that one is free to be responsible. The menu for choice varies; good and bad are not so clearly defined as they once were, neither are values or tradition, God's will or divine providence. I have to search out and test, to experience and judge, to act and accept the consequences. Christ died and rose to make me free. But that freedom is not just to say 'yes' or 'no' to someone else's formulation of the question; it is a freedom to see what salvation means not in a book of theology, but in the fresh possibilities of life and grace. The viability and vitality of what the church teaches emerges less in printed pronouncements than in the dynamism of living a good life in the world."

Even in my newly discovered awareness, I still had to wrestle with the church. I think I asked of it a kind of perfection I refused to require of myself. It was easy to critique the church by pointing out that the church Jesus founded was in the world as a pilgrim not a landlord, a teacher not a dictator; it was a church of prophets who believed what they preached and so preached with an understanding and an urgency that bore the stamp of saving conviction. The greatest apologetic for that church was not simply the coherence of doctrine, but the witness of its members living and dying with courage. That is a lot to measure up to, but

I allowed no leniency in my judgment of where and how often the church seemed to come up short.

During the years that followed that marked my journey—from New York to the University of Michigan and then to the University of Notre Dame—I receded into a kind of cultural Catholicism: I knew the teachings of the church even if I didn't always abide by them, or practice them, much less bear witness by living always with courage. In other words, I hid and pretended. I focused so much on how I wanted to ask—or not—the question that I lost touch with the real God I was trying to find.

Gradually, I grew more and more distant from the life of the church, and attention to God was mostly reserved for tense times, tragedies, and funerals. My hiding became so complete that I forgot I was hiding. Something else was happening, too. It was as though transparent scales grew over my eyes and I no longer cared to, or could, see with the eyes of faith. I could teach authentic Catholic doctrine and debate theological questions, but only in a disconnected way, as an intellectual exercise. My faith was more a deposit in my memory than a force in my life. And that seemed fine with me.

What this all amounted to is that I lived a fair portion of my life as a kind of baptized secular humanist. Not that this was bad, mind you, but just that it fostered in me a lifestyle that had no genuine moorings. Days and years dimmed both heart and sight. Finding my way in the garden was hard enough without trying to retrace my steps in search of the One who had been my companion decades before. I don't think hardness of heart had set in, but there is no doubt that my spiritual life had reduced itself to an occasional twinge, an instinctual kind of restless avoidance, and an easy postponement of any serious thought about it.

But it is God's reputation that he tracks people down because in some mysterious way, He needs each of us and all of us. Sinful and fickle as we are, we are His family and He will leave the ninety-nine good sheep to search for the lost one. Most of us don't hear Him calling us by name. He knows where we are better than we do and He accommodates our manner of knowing by sending both signs and the software necessary to read them.

I can describe, but not explain, what happened to me. Jeremy and Josh were both nearing the completion of their degrees at Notre Dame, and my wife, Jill, began to think about filling our emptying nest by adopting a so-called hard-to-place child. I agreed because it seemed a right and good thing to do. We contacted Catholic Charities and, when approved, chose a seven-week-old, biracial baby boy who we named Trevor Justice Langford. Over time it became apparent that he would spend his life coping with serious learning disabilities most likely caused by drug or alcohol consumption during pregnancy. For all of that, from the very beginning, Trevor's smile and sense of humor have been a constant substitute for physical coordination and the ability to speak. In a word, he has always been happy, and he has always brought happiness to others.

Soon after adopting Trevor, we decided to move to the country where we could enjoy the pleasures of privacy and quiet. We found an old farmhouse located on fifteen acres, well back from the road and only five miles from South Bend. I was so intent on warning off uninvited visitors that I put up a sign where our lane begins that said in effect, "If we don't know you're coming, turn around here." Except for a carload of Jehovah's Witnesses, the sign worked.

Trevor was three when Catholic Charities called to see whether we would be willing to adopt another biracial child, this time a girl. We said "yes." Emily Alice was three days old when we brought her home from the hospital. By then we were going to Mass on Sundays with regularity. We had found a little church where more than half the parishioners are African American, where the music is rousing, and the preaching often moving. We probably went out of curiousity, but the first time, and then the second and third, brought me to tears as echoes of old prayers and greetings to a God I had once known and cared about came pouring back. In a sense, the scales began to come off my eyes so that, dimly at first, I began again to see with the vision of faith. It was not long before that faith would drastically alter our lives.

One of the books we study in a course I teach at Notre Dame is *There Are No Children Here* by Alex Kotlowitz, the powerful account of two boys growing up in the Henry Horner housing project in Chicago. It seared the hearts of my students, and mine and Jill's too. We started talking about turning our haven into a place where inner-city children could come to relax and play, to be safe and made to feel good about themselves. In spite of opposition at the rezoning meeting raised by people who didn't want inner-city kids near their property, we obtained approval, incorporated as a tax-exempt organization, and began to develop our land into a camp for children. During the rezoning battle, when I was at my lowest ebb, a neighbor named Elson Fish called to say that he and his wife had prayed about the issue and that it was clear to them that this was God's work and that they should back us and battle with us. That was very powerful witness and I remember saying to myself, "So that's what faith looks like in the real world; you risk decades old relationships in order to stand up for what is right." I guess I knew that, but actually to see it was a kind of conversion experience for me. If you have faith, you can't leave it in the parlor; it has to be part of all you do, no matter what.

Through Kotlowitz and Trevor, Emily and Elson Fish, God found me and invited me to resume our walk. We argue sometimes, I pout sometimes, but on this little acre, I can be His eyes and arms, a sign of His love for children.

It is now eight years since inner-city agencies and centers started bringing children to the camp. We now average thirty-five hundred children and eighteen hundred volunteer visitors a year. Some of the children come as many as twenty-five or thirty days a year and we have come to know and love them like family. This is their country club, with a full basketball court, baseball diamond, volleyball court, bicycles for riding on trails through nine acres of woods, a clubhouse and a theater building, a huge sandbox, toys, games, tutors, mentors, and friends. The eyes of faith see minor miracles here all the time, starting with a delivery truck smashing my STAY OUT sign to bits as if a message was coming from God by United Parcel Service to the effect that this place is for all His children. Or the decision to go ahead with the basketball court even though we didn't have the money only to find a check in the envelope immediately under the one containing the winning bid from the asphalt paving company. The court and goals cost $5,050; the check was for $5,000. Just last week, we nearly ran out of food but two women appeared with a truckload of snacks and juices that will last for weeks.

Too many of the children who come here have stories that break your heart. The majority are from families that have experienced violence, drugs, poverty, and hopelessness. In the past two years, two of our campers have been murdered, two others have lost their mothers to murder. The dropout rate in the schools they attend is 48 percent. They carry more baggage at the age of ten than most people do in a lifetime. Some are in their third or fourth foster home, others are being raised by grandmothers because their parents are dead, in prison, or living far away.

Yet they come with resources, too. They are survivors; their instincts can detect genuine care and, though slowly, they respond to it deeply and with gratitude. Most look out for each other; nearly all display a sense of humor that rescues them from sadness or terror. Let me illustrate.

Markus is a ten-year-old who was here as part of a weekend for kids from the projects in Chicago. His body language, the way he walks, tells you he is old for ten. He sizes things up quickly; his eyes take in the situation and he is always alert, even edgy. He is from the *other* Chicago, the one that lives behind the tan face of tall buildings where, fifty years ago, blacks were moved into what was an urban equivalent of Indian reservations. Over time they became hell holes of death, despair, and destitution. As usual, the victims were blamed for their plight.

It doesn't take long to recognize that Markus is destined to be a leader. He is strong, determined, blessed with a sense of humor that he uses to shield himself in moments of sadness or discomfort in new surroundings. The other nine children in the group look up to him—a few with apprehension because he is volatile, most with admiration because he is forceful. Markus is one of the children we absolutely have to reach; he will play a key part in the battle between good and evil. But listen to the past twelve months of his story.

The project buildings are being demolished and the tenants are being moved to smaller and more dispersed public housing. Markus's building was one of the first to go and so his family moved out of the only home they had known. Of course it was a move up, but it also meant taking new bearings and discovering the street rules for the new, nearly as dangerous neighborhood.

During the school year, his teachers were determined to find out why he did so poorly in school. They convinced his mother to let him be tested. It was discovered that he is dyslexic. Just as more texts were scheduled, the principal came to his classroom and told him that he needed to go home. It was his aunt. She had just been murdered, thrown out of a fourth-floor window by her boyfriend.

Markus doesn't grieve; he says he's fine and shows smiles to prove it. The testing stops, but the teachers continue to breach the walls and salve his aches before they become callouses. Finally, he cries.

As the school year winds down, word comes that his school, a Catholic grade school in the inner city, is to be closed for financial reasons. One more hitching post for hope is pulled up and Markus is set free. What will happen to him now? Will other teachers care for him as these did? Two sides are already wrestling for his spirit—one reveals good manners, obvious care for his friends, who he shields and protects; the other shows a quick willingness to use force to claim his place. There he is, with his slightly cocky demeanor, his pick-comb lodged beneath his baseball cap, his eyes flashing, ready to smile—or to spring.

When we apply for grants, foundations ask for statistical evidence that the camp makes a difference. All we have as evidence are the sounds of happiness here every day, the line of children waiting week in and week out for our van to pick them up, the anecdotal evidence of memories created here, trust grown here, life enjoyed here. For us, it is enough.

What makes this place special, holy even, is that the college volunteers are as changed by it as much as are the children. One cannot meet these children without quickly coming to root for them and to care deeply about the economic, societal, educational, or familial problems, that must be faced at the level of governmental, corporate, and community awareness and reform. Some of our volunteers have changed their majors because they want to put their talents to work addressing the problems, whether in politics, social work, or teaching in inner-city schools. Some have committed to two years of service after graduation working with organizations in the inner cities. Many of them find a new way to define their faith because they sense that it is faith that makes this program run.

It is true that contrasting the smiling faces we see at the camp with the grim details of what some of them face can put one's faith to the test. Like Ivan in *The Brothers Karamazov*, one can easily find the suffering of children a stumbling block to belief in an all powerful and all good God. But God is not guilty. We are. And if we are hiding when God calls us in the garden, it is because we have too often averted our eyes from the poor, the homeless, the sick, and the disadvantaged. The great sin of our time is self-centeredness. It is that self-consumption that stops us from taking seriously the formula for happiness that Jesus laid out so clearly in his life and death. The paradox of Christian life is that the more you turn outward to others, the more you give, the more you empty yourself, the more you receive and are fulfilled. This means more than practicing random acts of kindness; it calls for a radical conversion in the way we live, the way we do business. The simple fact of the matter is that if we are going to walk with God in this fragile world, we have to do it by walking alongside and with our fellow sinners. We have to pull together in solidarity with every other human being on the earth. When one of us fails, we are all poorer. When one of us turns to the good, the whole community is better.

My years with the children and the volunteers have been God-given in every way. I cannot bring strong credentials to judgment day. But, like Cyrano de Bergerac, I do have one thing unsullied: my white plume is my abiding love for God's children. And this is my prayer:

Lord, I need to talk to you about the children.
Sometimes I wonder why you keep sending them
to us.
You surely know how we treat them, what we do
to them.
You have taken so many of them back before they
even owned a doll
Or dreamed of hitting a home run
Or thought about living long enough to graduate
from high school.
We have let them die of random gunshots,
starvation, drugs, and disease,
Of loneliness, abuse, and despair.
A friend who is a counselor at a local elementary
school told me
That in the past two weeks he has dealt with
Two suicide notes, three fifth graders who have
joined a notorious gang,
And more than a few fourth and fifth graders who
are sexually active.
What have we done . . . or not done . . . to your
children? Who can they trust?
What must you be suffering,
You, who still a child, amazed the elders in the
temple
You, who though exhausted at the end of a day of
preaching and teaching,
Ordered your apostles not to prevent the children
from you.

And it was You, Lord, who told us that unless we
become like children
We cannot enter the kingdom.
I think what you meant was unless we speak
the truth,
Unless we trust and dream and hope and love
Unless we play and laugh and reach out to others

With both hands like children are meant to do,
we cannot be ready to see You.
Surely You didn't mean that you want us to be like
so many children today—afraid, alone neglected,
molested, threatened, streetwise,
Suspicious, hopeless.
How can we be childlike if children cannot be
children anymore?

Show us the way, Lord.
Start at the beginning. Teach us how to
see ourselves,
Our actions and omissions,
Through a child's eyes. Remind us:
All children are our children
And we are all your children.
Help us.

IV
AND FAITH WILL LIGHT THE WAY
THEODORE M. HESBURGH, C.S.C.

In my eighty-five years, I have logged nearly twenty million miles trying to walk with God in this world that is His creation. I have been friends with paupers and princes, popes and professors, protesters and politicians. It often seemed to me that there were not enough hours in a day to do everything I might do on this pilgrimage. My aim has been to bring faith to bear on the problems that try to crush the lives of the vast majority of people on this planet. Faith has always been the lens through which I focused on what I saw and sensed, what I wished for and worked for, whether as a member of some high-powered commission or in a simple encounter with a campesino family in rural Chile.

I have never considered myself holy. One need only read the great spiritual writers to understand that mystical union with God is a gift not given to everyone, not even everyone who has vowed to live a life dedicated to God. But I can say that I tried to cooperate with the grace given me and to serve the Lord in my work as president of the University of Notre Dame, as an adviser to presidents and popes, or as a member of commissions that dealt with issues such as civil rights, atomic energy, world hunger, or reconciliation after Vietnam. I was there as a representative of my faith and that never failed to inform my views no matter how seemingly secular the issues or experts appeared to be.

I can say that, because if there is any center in my life, anything that is inseparable from my identity, it is my priesthood. That is the ground of my being. In the midst of a busy schedule, almost incessant study and preparation for commission meetings, flights, phone calls, talks, and similar responsibilities, it would have been easy—and perhaps forgivable—to omit the daily recitation of the divine office, readings from the Scriptures and prayers that change daily as part of the liturgical year. Sometimes it might have been convenient to forego the celebration of Mass. But I don't think I ever willingly missed praying the office, and with only two or three exceptions, I celebrated Mass every day in my nearly sixty years as a priest. The steadfastness of these devotions every day, together with the practices that go with belonging to a religious community and a daily examination of conscience to see how you are progressing in the task of becoming a better person, all combine to make one mindful every day that no matter what pressures or deliberations, or challenges had to be faced, they would have behind them a will and care firmly rooted in the love of God and humankind, and a commitment that comes from deep within one's own identity.

Some of this lifelong understanding of the importance of daily practice started when I was a child. I always said the rosary when I went to bed. My mother used to tell me, "Just start it. If you fall asleep, your guardian angel will finish it for you."

The Mass is at the center of my life with God. No matter where I was or how difficult the logistics, I always built my day around the celebration of the Eucharist. I have said Mass in a lot of strange and exotic places over the years, from the South Pole, to fifty thousand feet over the Amazon jungle, to seven hundred feet under the ocean in a submarine. One time, after I had flown from Alaska to Louisiana and arrived at about five o'clock in the morning, I asked the airline representative if there was an empty office where I could say Mass. He took me to an office that had a window looking out toward one of the runways. I was just finishing Mass when a baggage worker saw me through the window and came in to see who I was and exactly what I was doing there. He said, "Hey, what are you doing?" I replied, "I am saying Mass." He looked around the room and, seeing no one else, said "For who?" I said, "For the whole blessed world, including you!" Usually before or right after sessions of the governmental commissions, I would invite the other commission members, most of whom were not Catholic, to join me for the Mass. Often they did. My own sense of the universal inclusiveness of Mass was deepened by reading the works of Teilhard de Chardin. In his *Hymn of the Universe* there is a passage that captures this well:

> I, your priest, will make the whole earth my altar and on it will offer you all the labors and sufferings of the world.
>
> Over there, on the horizon, the sun has just touched with light the outermost fringe of the eastern sky. Once again, beneath this moving sheet of fire, the living surface of the earth wakes and trembles, and once again begins in fearful travail. I will place on my paten, O God, the harvest to be won by this renewal of labor. Into my chalice I shall pour all the sap which is to be pressed out this day from the earth's fruits.
>
> One by one Lord, I see and I love all those you have given me to sustain and charm my life. One by one also I number all those who make up that other beloved family which has gradually surrounded me, its unity fashioned out of the most disparate elements, with affinities of the heart, of scientific research and of thought. And again one by one—more vaguely it is true, yet all inclusively—I call before me the whole vast anonymous army of living humanity;

those who surround me and support me though I do
not know them; those who come and those who go;
above all, those who in office, laboratory and factory,
through their vision of truth or despite their error,
truly believe in the progress of earthly reality and
who today will take up again their impassioned pursuit of the light. . . .

Receive, O Lord, this all-embracing host which
your whole creation, moved by your magnetism, offers you at the dawn of a new day.

This bread, our toil, is of itself, I know, but an im-
mense fragmentation; this wine, our pain, is no more,
I know than a draught that dissolves. Yet in the very
depths of this formless mass you have implanted . . . a
desire, irresistible, hallowing, which makes us cry out,
believer and unbeliever alike, "Lord, make us one."[1]

That says, better than I ever could, why the Mass, in its particularity and universality, has always been at the heart of my
spiritual life.

The point I want to make is that walking with God
down every corridor, every day, means that you find a way
explicitly to tie your identity to your faith so that you know
who you are and what you stand for—and so does everybody else. One doesn't need to be ordained a priest to do
that. Decades before the Second Vatican Council reaffirmed
the priesthood of the laity, I wrote my dissertation for the
doctorate in theology on the fact that the mandate for social action comes to the laity not from the hierarchy but
from the sacraments of baptism and confirmation. We are, all
of us, in some way priests. My view of "church" has always
been that Christ is the head and we are the members of his
mystical body, entrusted with the privilege and duty to
bring His love and care to the world. This understanding rejects exclusiveness; it is open to all. It sees the sacred as the

leaven in the world. It urges us to feed, clothe, console, inspire, and accompany others on their journey through this fragile world. But to do this, we need to remind ourselves every single day of our identity as Christians. That should make us more, not less, committed to working for the social changes that announce the kingdom of God on earth.

The central way I carry my faith with me, having anchored it in the Mass, divine office, and prayer, is to see myself as a member of the mystical body of Christ, constantly in need of guidance, inspiration, and enlightenment from the Holy Spirit. Jesus promised to send the Holy Spirit to be with us always. I have long been in the habit of saying "Veni Sancte Spiritus"—"Come Holy Spirit." It is my first prayer in the morning and my last prayer at night. Its fifteen verses are both beautiful and powerful. Whether asked for counsel by a world leader or a freshman in college, I never answer without saying "Come Holy Spirit" in my mind. If there is any explanation for landing on my feet over the years, or coming up with a workable solution to a problem, it is thanks to that. If there is any secret to my life spiritually, it is that I ask the Holy Spirit for the light to know what has to be done and for the grace to be able to do it.

Having said this, I need to add that I felt free to call on the Holy Spirit because I never relied on that prayer as a way to avoid doing my homework. Before you can offer a good answer to a pressing problem, you need to have a clear understanding of the problem itself and then to make certain you foresee the ramifications of the solution you propose. Principles can be perfectly true in the abstract, but more than a little complicated as they are applied to concrete problems. For example, a theologian addressing moral issues arising from science or technology needs first of all to understand the science so as to have the problems and its parameters framed correctly.

I never stopped studying on my journey through life. Whether the subject matter was higher education, social justice, atomic energy, peace, or poverty, I felt an obligation to learn everything I could from whatever source. The work of a high-powered commission doesn't consist of sitting around a table and discussing ideas; the real work is in the preparation—the study of reams of documents and research reports that bear on the issue at hand. Addressing social issues requires both the mind and the heart—intelligence as well as empathy and compassion. And, I would add, the grace of God as well.

My strong sense of social justice and human dignity as universal rights came first and foremost from the teachings of the Catholic Church. The papal encyclicals on basic human rights in society are extremely powerful documents. They provide both a vision and a blueprint for progress toward genuine human liberation. When we see someone like Mother Teresa put those principles into practice, we begin to understand their power. When I first came to Notre Dame in 1934, I met a fellow by the name of Vince McAloon. He exemplified the attitude I have tried to follow in my own life. Every evening, Vince would borrow a truck and load it with containers of food left over from the dining hall on campus. Then he would drive to a place near the railroad yard known as "the jungle," a place where so-called bums would gather after jumping off of freight cars. Vince brought them warm food because he saw it as his Christian duty to feed the hungry. He fed other people too and tried to help them find scarce jobs. After graduation, Vince went on a pilgrimage across Europe, from Portugal to Rome. He would stop at farmhouses along the way and ask to sleep in the barn. In return for some soup or bread, he offered to pray for the host family as part of his pilgrimage.

I like to think that Vince's example and the metaphor of his pilgrimage could serve as a way of seeing how my life unfolded as a priest who tried to serve as best he could. I served as an adviser to six presidents and four popes and that required that I delve deeply into the human condition to see what might be done to raise the level of human living conditions and hopes. As a member of the board of the Rockefeller Foundation, I saw the worldwide problem of hunger. The facts cried out for drastic action. Some 80 percent of the people in the world are malnourished, while 20 percent have more than they could ever need. The foundation started programs all over the world to improve crops and increase their yields, to reduce disease in animals raised for food, and to improve sanitary conditions as well as water supplies. These programs led to dramatic improvements, including a 600 percent increase in the world's food supply. But there is still much to do. Hunger still haunts too many people around the globe and even here at home.

Pope Paul VI was on the mark when he said, "If you want peace, work for justice." If 80 percent of the world's resources are in the hands of 20 percent of the population, that is a terrible situation. And the United States is not immune to it. We have more freedoms than anyone in the world, we have the freedom and right to choose our own officials, access to education and employment, legal rights that make us the most just society in the world. But we still have millions of blacks, Hispanics, poor whites, and others who do not share in our bounty, who do not have genuine access to quality education, proper nutrition, adequate medical care, decent housing, judicial equality, or the ramp to the communication superhighway. There is no doubt that we have made real progress in the past four or five decades in desegregation, affirmative action, judicial reform, and immunization of the young. But we are still no where near where we need to be on these crucial components of happiness. We are still on the verge of slipping into a disparity between the haves and have-nots that is not far from that of a Third World nation.

When you add globalization to this picture, you begin to understand the image that much of the rest of the world has of the United States. Whatever happens here is known immediately around the world. People everywhere can see our excesses—the resorts and lifestyles of the rich and famous, people with multiple mansions—one for each season of the year—and they cannot see why we have so much and they have so little of the basic things, forget the luxuries, that make life worth living. Given the gap between the rich and poor, there should be no real mystery about the causes of war, revolution, violence, crime, and hatred. It is not enough to respond, "Well, that's the way life is . . . no one guaranteed it would be fair." That kind of attitude is exactly what led some people in other parts of the world to celebrate the real and symbolic disaster inflicted on the United States on September 11. People who live in tin shacks and drink muddy water, people who have no power, no avenue to change their state in life, people who yearn unsuccessfully for a few moments of serenity and safety, such people have a difficult time lamenting a tragedy that happens to the richest people on the earth.

So what is the conclusion? How does one walk with God in such a world? It is pretty clear that we need more than words to change the world. Nothing short of a new and widespread commitment to some well-tested traditions and truth will do. Peace will not come until social justice is a reality. The life and words of Jesus are the clarion call. The parable of the Good Samaritan, the Beatitudes, the vivid example of giving up his life for his friends all tell important truths. So does his response to the rich young man seeking to be part of the kingdom: "Go, sell what you have, give to the poor, and come follow me." All of this points to a solidarity that alone can settle the world. We are our brother's and our sister's keeper; and everyone is our brother and sister. It is as simple and as complex as that.

I really feel that I was never alone, that I did walk with God through this world, trying to help improve the situations of the underprivileged in our country and abroad. One of the important strengths that came from my faith was an unshakeable hope based on Christ's promise that good will someday prevail. For me, faith was and is an antidote to disillusionment; it lets us see beyond the limited vision that tells us it is unreasonable to go on trying, that the odds against success are simply too great. We need to believe in the possibility of change for the better. Circumstances enabled me to be part of the effort on a large scale. Certainly governmental and foundation-supported programs can direct massive resources that are necessary in any overall strategy to improve the quality of life for those who are suffering and in need. But material resources and abstract good will are not enough to win the day. That will take people at every level to embrace the Beatitudes. Think what the world would be like if everyone chose to live by these precepts:

Happy are the poor in spirit:
theirs is the kingdom of heaven.
Happy are the gentle:
they shall have the earth for their heritage.
Happy are those who mourn:
they shall be comforted.
Happy are those who hunger and thirst for what
is right:
they shall be satisfied.
Happy the merciful:
they shall have mercy shown them.
Happy the pure of heart:
they shall see God.

> Happy the peacemakers:
> they shall be called children of God.
> Happy those who are persecuted in the cause of
> right:
> theirs is the kingdom of heaven.
> (Matt. 5, 3–10: The Jerusalem Bible)

It is at this level, the micro level, involving the efforts of individuals that the fight for social justice will be won. Think of it: if we ever get to the point where every Christian, Jew, and Muslim decided to make the commitments called for in the Beatitudes, we can change the face of the world almost overnight. And it is happening. Quietly, massively, it is happening. I see it on the Notre Dame campus like never before. The vast majority of our students are involved in service commitments to the homeless, the infirm, the aged, inner-city children, the developmentally handicapped, and our local community is much transformed by it. A remarkable and growing percentage of our graduates devote the first year or two as volunteers in various faith-based organizations, as well as the Peace Corps, AmeriCorps, and others. The same is true at colleges and universities around the country. This new volunteerism exists even at the high school level and a record of service is required on the application forms of the best colleges and universities in the land.

If we all began to walk more consciously with God in his world, the world would soon be less fragile. We cannot simply celebrate the spirit of volunteerism among the young. Each of us needs to find a way to help, no matter how full our daily time card already is. I cannot remember a time when I did not have a dozen things to do at once. As time went on, I learned how to give up the less important activities in order to do the important ones with full, undivided attention. I learned that you need not worry about what you just did; when you leave it, leave it. Don't worry about what you have to do tomorrow; there will be time enough for that tomorrow. Give the present your full attention. The real secret to meeting many demands is possessing inner peace. No matter what problems, pressures, or tensions, we will not be much good unless we think clearly and act calmly and resolutely.

I truly believe that, with faith in God and in our fellow humans, we can together aim for the heights of human endeavor, and that we can reach them, too. Through all the miles and the moments of my walk, I have felt the presence of the One who is our creator and redeemer. What I hope my life might have to say, especially to the young, is this: He believed, he hoped, he tried, he failed often enough, but with God's grace he often accomplished more than he rationally could have dreamed. He gave witness to those wonderful words of Scripture: "God has chosen the weak of the world to confound the strong." So we are weak. No matter.

NOTE

1. Pierre Teilhard de Chardin, *Hymn of the Universe*, trans. Simon Bartholomew (New York: Harper & Row, 1965).

V
ON THE STREETS OF A FRAGILE WORLD
Virgil Elizondo

I was born and raised in San Antonio, Texas, and grew up walking the city's downtown streets as if they were my own backyard. There were always plenty of people of all ages and backgrounds walking around, but there never seemed to be anything special about the place.

It was a totally different scene when after many years I returned to the downtown as rector of San Fernando Cathedral. As I walked the same streets I had known growing up, I started to become aware of many things that I had never noticed before. Besides the downtown being somewhat run-down, the many closed stores and especially the closed movie houses I had enjoyed so much, there was something else that was very different. Maybe it had always been there, but I had never noticed it before.

Certainly there were many more tourists than locals walking around. This was indeed something new. But there was something else. I started to notice the presence of many homeless people, some drug peddlers and many male and female prostitutes. I suspect they had been around all the time, but I had never been aware of them before. These people made the downtown their home and therefore they were my parishioners. I was supposed to be their pastor, but I had no preparation for dealing with them. So what should I do? How should I deal with them? Should I just avoid them? Should I chastise them and condemn them for their immorality? Should I go to the City Council and demand that they pass laws to "clean up the city." I really did not know what to do.

So, in desperation, I went to my favorite counselor. After I had closed down the cathedral for the night and had it all to myself, I went to pray before the Blessed Sacrament. I have always experienced a great source of energy and wisdom emanating from the tabernacle. Call it magic if you wish, call it superstition or whatever. To me, since I was a little child, it has been the real presence of Jesus waiting to enter into deep conversation with me. I love to just kneel or sit there in silence and let my mind wander wherever it goes, I don't try to control or guide it, I just let myself be in the presence of the Master. Sometimes I even fall into a peaceful sleep. There is an incredible peace and serenity and illumination that gradually takes over—sometimes. Other times, its just a terrific place to truly rest and relax.

There in the silence of the night, the cathedral glittering with hundreds of vigil lights burning and the city lights illuminating the stained glass windows, answers to my pastoral dilemma began to become clear to me. How did Jesus deal with persons similar to the ones I was encountering? How did he deal with the Samaritan woman? With the Centurion who wanted his boy to be healed? With the public sinners and prostitutes he encountered?

Jesus did not chastise the people in the margins who were looked upon as the public sinners of society; he entered into conversation with them, treated them as persons, befriended them, and invited them into his company. By so doing, he enabled them to recognize what society had denied them: their fundamental human dignity and infinite worth! This was the beginning of their change, this was the "good news"—they were not worthless whores or bums, but human beings! Jesus was not afraid to shock and scandalize all the good and pious people of his time who found it so easy to judge, classify, and condemn but so impossible to accept, understand, and appreciate.

Who is not broken in some way or another? Wounded people need healing, not additional bruises. The healing begins when I encounter someone who does not judge or condemn me, who does not ridicule or chastise me, who does not walk away from me or classify me as scum. The healing begins when I encounter someone who simply accepts me, listens to my story, and is willing to accompany me in the life I find myself in. Often it is a life without any joy or satisfaction, but it is a life that I have been entrapped in.

All of a sudden it was very clear what I had to do. I should simply befriend these people who walked the streets. They could not really understand me. One of them even offered me a clergy discount. Gradually they became friendlier and I started to discover some of the most painful stories I had ever heard. I discovered why Jesus had such a special place in his heart for prostitutes, why they hold such a privileged place in the gospel narratives. They are not the public sinners they are made out to be by hypocritical societies, but the very victims of this society. I could share with you many stories, but space limits me to two. One of a woman prostitute and one of a male prostitute. The names have been changed, the details are true.

Carmen was a bit older, but a very beautiful woman. There was an incredible charm and dignity about her. Her husband had been from a very rich family in Mexico and she had come from a very poor family in Mexico. They had been married a few years and had three beautiful children. His family had never approved of their marriage. He died suddenly.

During the wake, she overheard his family conspiring as to how they were going to take the children away from her and chase her out on the street. She simply did not belong to "our class" and the children would be far better off without her. After all, they were very young and would be told that both of their parents had died early. They would never know about her or her lowly status.

She was deeply troubled, in desperation and totally confused. Immediately after the funeral, she took the children and fled to a friend's house. She was frantic and had no idea what to do. She went to the basilica to ask the Virgin for a miracle. On the way out, a woman stopped her and asked if she would be interested in well-paying employment in the United States. Of course! What kind of work? Entertainment, being a social hostess at events, accompanying people. It sounded great. The miracle had come quickly. The woman was even willing to give her a substantial cash advance and give her time to work things out and even arrange for her passport to the United States.

Through her friends, she was able to get her children into a Catholic school in a small rural town away from Mexico City. She made all the arrangements quickly and was soon on her way to New Orleans. She was full of excitement and expectation. Little did she suspect what was in store for her.

It was a totally different story when she arrived. Her passport was quickly taken way from her, she was housed in a prison-like place and instructed on the duties of her new job: to render sexual favors to the men who came around. There was no doubt, this was a high-class place and there would be good money involved, the money she needed to educate her children well. She hated the life she was entering into, but it was the necessary sacrifice for the sake of her children. It was horrible at first, but she learned to distance herself emotionally from her work—it soon became no different from sewing clothes in a sweat shop or picking crops in the fields, except the pay was much better and this enabled her to take good care of her children and even provide for her aging parents.

When she became older, she was dismissed. This was the only work she knew. She had traveled through several cities and ended up in San Antonio. She was very proud of her children and showed me treasured pictures of them. They had no idea what she was doing, but loved her visits when she would take them many gifts and clothing from the United States. I'll never forget some of her comments: "I did not choose this life, life chose it for me." She was not proud of her work, she lived in deep shame, yet she was proud and grateful that she still had her children, that her children had not been taken away from her, that she had given them a good education, and that they would never have to work at the type of work she had been forced into.

She was a great inspiration to me. The incredible sacrifice that one is willing to make for the sake of others. To others she might have been a scandal, to me she was an inspiration, a sacrament of God's love for us. After all, wasn't the Son of God willing to take on the sins of the world for our salvation?

The other was a young man named Joe. He was a very attractive young man who had another job during the day but liked to walk the streets at night looking for older men. We gradually became friends and one day he told me his story. He was the son of a mistress and a father who would not recognize him as his son. He knew who his father was, but his father would not acknowledge him or his birthright.

He had only had physical contact with his father twice in his life. Once when he was a young child, the father had spent the night with his mother and while he was drinking his morning coffee, Joe playfully had hit the cup and spilled it over his lap. The man became so angered and violent that he slapped the boy so hard that he burst his eardrum. Thus Joe is deaf in one ear.

A few years later, the man's legitimate son started making fun of Joe in the school playground for being a bastard son. Joe became angry and got into a big fight with his half-brother. That night, the father came to Joe's house to give him a whipping for daring to insult his real son! He gave him such a strapping that for several days it was hard for him to sit down.

Why was Joe walking the streets looking for older men? As he told me, he liked women, but at nights he felt he was searching for the embrace of the father, the embrace he had never received from his father. He had seen other fathers playing with their children, hugging and kissing them. He had really wanted this, but he had never had it. The only thing he really wanted in life was to someday have his father recognize him, put his arm around him, and simply call him "my son." He wasn't asking for anything else, but the basic recognition that he was his son.

Knowing who his father was and longing for the recognition of being his son was his painful wound and the source of the deep loneliness that he tried to heal and compensate for in the streets of San Antonio. He told me he really didn't enjoy the sex, but he loved the embrace and the caresses he would receive from the older men whose advances he would accept. He would sort of brag: "I'm pretty picky, I turn down most of the advances, I can tell a weirdo a mile away."

I didn't want to scare him away by preaching to him too quickly. Gradually I told him how Jesus might have gone through something similar since people did not know who his earthly father was and I was sure there must have been plenty of rumors. He was fascinated by this. As the conversations continued, we gradually started to talk about Jesus' fascination with God as "Abba" as "Papacito" as

"Daddy." God is the ultimate Father of all of us and even the ones who do not have an earthly father to recognize them as their children, still have God as the loving Father who calls them by name, embraces them, and says: "This is my beloved child."

Joe enrolled in our Rite of Christian Initiation for Adults and in going through the program experienced a real rebirth, it was a real resurrection experience. He found incredible healing and liberation in saying the "Our Father" and one day he told me: "It really feels good to call you father." I don't think I have ever received a more beautiful compliment. But even better yet was his simple confessional statement one day. In a somewhat laughing way, he stated: "I'm sleeping better these days, I don't have to walk the streets at night anymore."

He cried great tears of joy the night of his baptism, for him it was a real death, a thorough cleansing/purification of his previous life. He joined the choir, became active in the parish, found a beautiful girlfriend, and today is happily married and very dedicated to his children. "I never want my children to suffer what I have suffered."

I never asked him to stop his streetwalking. By simply walking with him through his life, never condemning but only seeking to understand with compassion, gradually inviting him into alternatives he had not suspected even existed, he found a new life! Incredible as it sounds to many, the simple but profound recognition that God is our Father, my Father who loves me beyond what any human father could love was the "Good News" which he had never known and that brought redemption to him.

I often wondered how many Joes and Carmens there are walking around the streets, selling drugs, joining gangs, selling themselves. I have met many kids in detention centers who have never had the loving embrace of a parent or the experience of a caring home. Many have only experienced beatings, insults, and rejection.

Many of the children who came to catechism at San Fernando Cathedral were from these types of backgrounds. Some were living with grandparents because both of their parents were in jail or had left them behind to go find employment somewhere else. Some were children of the same mother but of different fathers and were not too sure who their own father was. Single mothers were quite common. I would tell our catechists that, of course, I wanted the children to learn about God, Jesus, Mary, and the saints, but most of all, I wanted the children to have an experience of being radically welcomed, accepted, valued, and loved! This is what church is about, creating a new space where anyone and everyone will feel valued and welcomed!

I would often end the day by spending time with the Lord in the Blessed Sacrament. He is very real to me. Often my stories did not have happy endings. There were many tragic ones. But I kept hearing his voice telling me: "I didn't succeed too well at first, they even abandoned me at the end, so just stay in there, keep loving them and loving them even more."

It seems incredible to me that the more we advance in our world, the more fragile our world seems to become. Upward mobility seems to lead to personal disintegration while misery, abandonment, and poverty equally destroy the human spirit. We are indeed rushing to perfect the modern culture of death! Great capitals are made at the cost of cheating the people and impoverishing the masses. Modern technology deprived more and more people of decent work. The contradictions are legion. Great and even miraculous medical advances are made at the same time as more and more people are denied even the most basic medical benefits. More and more crops are produced while more and more of the world's people die early because of starvation. Billionaires multiply while poverty enslaves millions.

Yet the great miracle is not that we believe in God. Who else can we go to that still has credibility? The great miracle is that God still believes in us! We do so many crazy, stupid, irrational things, and yet God keeps believing in us and calling us to build a better world. There is no time to waste. We are, all of us, called to walk with God in our homes, in public, in the workplace, and, yes, on the streets.

Part Two

BELIEVING IS SEEING

"Depth does not have to be translated into Father or into Lord and King. God is height, but also depth; transcendence, but also intimacy. God is what Dietrich Bonhoeffer called 'the beyond' in the midst of our life."

—Diana Eck, *Encounters with God*

VI

WATCHING FOR GOD
Jürgen Moltmann

It was astonishing: all over the world, a response to the terrorist attacks in New York and Washington on September 11, 2001, was public prayer. And not just in religious America either. In secular Germany, too, people met in marketplaces and school playgrounds to pray in silence, and to light candles, and to put down flowers as a sign of their sympathy and their grief. In Berlin so many people streamed into the cathedral that the pastor had to hold a spontaneous service. In incredulous horror, people called on the God they had forgotten for so long. Jürgen Habermas, the philosopher of critical theory and a member of the Frankfurt School, calls himself irreligious; but in his speech in the Paulskirche in Frankfurt he called for the lost certainties of faith. But this public wave of religious feeling didn't last long. The search for the certainty of faith in prayer was not followed up. Modern rationalism didn't find the way to God. Why didn't these religious feelings lead to anything? Because although we still associate religion with praying, we no longer associate praying with watching. In prayer we search for a hidden God above us; but we no longer watchfully expect the coming God ahead of us. When we look for God, we close our eyes to the terrors of the world. But blind prayer is not prayer in Christ's name. The important thing is the watching.

"WATCH AND PRAY," "PRAY AND WATCH"

What else is Christian spirituality except this watching and praying, watching prayerfully and praying watchfully? Prayer never stands by itself. It is always bound up with watching. Here I want to talk about the watching which goes with true praying, and to which true prayer is supposed to lead us. Praying is good, but watching is better.

Modern men and women think that people who pray no longer belong properly to this world at all. They already have one foot in the world beyond. Strong men often think that praying is something for old women who have nothing left to them but the rosary or the hymnbook.

It is true enough that our body language when we pray doesn't particularly suggest watchfulness. We close our eyes and look into ourselves, so to speak. We fold our hands, so as to collect our thoughts. We kneel down, lower our eyes— even cast ourselves down with our faces to the ground. No one who sees us would get the impression that this is a collection of especially watchful people. Isn't it, rather, blind trust in God which is expressed in attitudes of prayer and meditation like this? Why do we shut our eyes? Don't we need much more an open-eyed mysticism? But what are we supposed to watch for? For whom are we supposed to watch? And against whom are we supposed to be watchful?

"COULD YOU NOT WATCH WITH ME ONE HOUR?"

The most impressive story about watching is also Jesus' hardest hour, the night in Gethsemane. The heading in Luther's Bible is: "The Struggle in Gethsemane"; for this denotes Jesus' inner struggle with God-forsakenness. His prayer to the God he calls Abba, dear Father, is not answered. The cup of eternal death does not pass him by. The night of what Martin Buber called the eclipse of God falls on him and on those who are his, and on this world. That is why in this hour Christ began "to be greatly distressed and troubled," says Mark; "to be sorrowful and troubled," writes Matthew. "My soul is very sorrowful, even to death," he tells the disciples. Earlier, he had often withdrawn and prayed all night long by himself in the hills. But in this hour he is afraid of being alone with his God, and he begs his disciples: "Stay here and watch." Jesus prays and struggles with the dark and mysterious will of his God, and his disciples are supposed to take over the watching, but his disciples fall into a deep, oblivious sleep. "Simon Peter, are you asleep? Could you not watch with me one hour?" This scene, so saddening for Jesus and so shaming for the disciples, is repeated three times. Jesus wrestles with the dark, rejecting side of God, and the stifling unconsciousness of sleep descends on the disciples until the night is past and the day of Golgotha begins, into which Jesus goes actively and resolutely: "Get up, let us be going. My betrayer is at hand." We all know what happens after that. But what strange kind of sleep was it, which overcame the truest of the true?

In the monastery of San Marco in Florence, there is a remarkable fresco in one of the cells, painted by Fra Angelico. It is the scene in Gethsemane. Jesus is praying, the disciples are sleeping; but two people are watching at Jesus' side, two women. The one looks wide-eyed in the direction of Jesus as she prays. The other is reading the Bible. It is Martha and Mary. They are watching with Jesus, and over him, in the hour of his God-forsakenness.

Why do the disciples fall asleep? If the Master whom they have followed without fear and trembling begins to tremble and fear himself, some cruel and inscrutable danger must surely be lurking. What danger? Through his healings of the sick, Jesus had communicated the nearness of God in ways that could be seen and felt—through the senses. But for the disciples this nearness now evidently turns into God's absence. Their feeling that God had found them is turned upside down: it becomes a sense of being lost without anything to cling to. It is as if they have been felled by some blow. Their reaction is numbness, and the sleep of hopelessness. We know what this is like. Impending danger can stimulate us, but danger with no way out numbs us, and we take flight into sleep, a sleep which protects us from what is unendurable. It is not a natural, refreshing sleep. It is the petrifying of all our senses, which makes us sick. Our eyes are open, but we no longer see anything. Our ears are open, but we are deaf and hear nothing. We are apathetic, and feel nothing. When danger threatens, we spontaneously and involuntarily "play dead."

SPIRITUAL PARALYSES TODAY

The paralyzing sleep which fell on Jesus' disciples in the night of God in Gethsemane was not their problem only. It is our problem today, too. How do we react to unknown dangers?

For millions of years, our consciousness has learned to react to the most widely differing dangers in life-supporting ways. How? Through the fear which keeps us wakeful and all our senses keyed up, so that we can encounter whatever threatens us. In our civilizations there are inbuilt securities for our survival, from lightning conductors to dikes against storm tides, securities with which we can control the dangers we are aware of.

But today there are dangers which are present without our perceiving them. In 1986, in the catastrophe in the Chernobyl nuclear power station, deadly radioactivity was released which we can neither smell nor taste nor see. It contaminated huge stretches of Europe, and, up to now, has cost the lives of 150,000 people. In these nuclear dangers our senses let us down. Our highly developed danger-antennae don't react to these perils. "Our nuclear power stations are completely safe," we are told, year after year. But no insurance company is prepared to insure a nuclear power plant against a meltdown.

The nuclear threat still exists, even if hardly anyone gets excited about it any more, and even if the chances of a nuclear conflict are not particularly great at present—at least not nearly as great as they were during the East–West confrontation in the so-called Cold War.

But for all that, we are still sitting on the bombs. More than twenty thousand atomic bombs in the East and the West are still on hand, "as solution to the question of the human race"; for, after a nuclear winter, there will no longer be any human life on this earth. In Europe, during the last century, two world wars taught us what an invasion with hundreds of thousands of soldiers means. But what an attack with thousands of nuclear warheads would mean we do not know, and we cannot begin to conceive. It exceeds the bounds of our imagination. So we repress the nuclear peril that still exists, and behave as if it weren't there; or, we repress our knowledge of it, and we do not permit ourselves to harbor nuclear anxieties anymore. The new American plans for a missile defense shield in space leave us as cold as do the Russian missile torpedoes. We have become inured to it all.

The way we react to the growing ecological crises is no different. We don't perceive the destruction of the ozone layer with the help of our senses. It doesn't touch us directly.

The connection between the increase in ultraviolet rays and skin cancer has been proved, but only statistically; so, no one needs to feel personally concerned. The time that elapses between cause and effect is too long for us to perceive it directly. So the ecological crises also leave us relatively cold. We suppress our knowledge of them because "we don't want to know": we don't want to know about the damage we are inflicting today on the already damaged world our children and grandchildren are going to live in.

The growing climatic changes are much more threatening than we have assumed up to now. According to the Third Report of the International Panel of Climate Change 2001, global warming must definitely be put down to human activity. In the next forty years temperatures are going to rise by two to five degrees Celsius. Ocean levels will rise, the river estuaries will be flooded, many islands in the Pacific will disappear, there will continually be "natural" catastrophes, which are in fact man-made. In the year 2050 there will be about 150 million climate refugees. But the United States is not prepared to sign the Kyoto Protocol because, as President Bush explained with naive frankness, "the American way of life" must be preserved; and, as we know, this way of life is characterized by its extensive use of energy and even more extensive atmospheric pollution. Their eyes are open but they do not see; their ears are open but they do not hear—until catastrophe overtakes them. And then they will swear: this is all new to us.

To put it briefly, the more we know about these new global dangers the less we want to know about them. We are not merely "unwilling" to feel pain, grief, and sympathy; with the best will in the world, we are incapable of feeling them. We don't see anymore, don't hear anymore, don't feel with other people anymore. We register things, but we don't take them in. Perhaps we are becoming unconsciously cynical, and are throwing ourselves into the modern fun society in which "I'm all right Jack" and our own "today" are all that matter: "after us the deluge." But that means that we are no longer aware of true reality. We live only in our own dreams, and we think that our illusions of reality are reality itself. And that, again, means that we are not wide awake to reality. We are asleep in the agreeable dreams of our fantasy worlds.

What is especially seductive and fascinating in these wishful worlds of ours is our own image of ourselves. We see ourselves as we should like to be. As in the fairytale, "Mirror, mirror on the wall" is always supposed to tell us that we are "the fairest one of all"—or the strongest, or the cleverest, or whatever we like best. But then there come moments of profound horror such as struck America after the terrorist attack on September 11, 2001, when we ask in fear or anger: "Why do they hate us so much?" The answer is a simple one: go out and ask the people who are evidently suffering under the policies of your government. Learn to see yourselves in the mirror of other people's eyes, and especially the eyes of the victims. That is painful, and hurts the image of ourselves we cherish so much; but it helps us to wake up out of our dreams and to come face to face with reality.

WATCH AND PRAY

My old Bible lexicon tells me that "watching discerns the danger—praying brings help from God." That is true; but all the same, it is not quite as simple as that.

What are we seeking when we pray?

When we pray, we are seeking the reality of God. We are breaking out of the Hall of Mirrors of our own wishes and illusions, in which we are imprisoned. That means that we undo the straitjacket that imprisons our feelings. We try to break out of the apathy that holds us in an iron grasp. If in prayer we seek the reality of God's world, then that is the exact opposite of "the opium of the people." Prayer is more like the beginning of a cure for the numbing addictions of the secular world.

In prayer we wake up to the world as it is spread out before God in all its heights and depths. We perceive the sighing of our fellow creatures, and we hear the cries of the created beings that have fallen on deaf ears. We hear the song of praise of the blossoming spring, and chime in with it. We feel the divine love for life which allows pain to touch us to the quick, and kindles joy. So real prayer to God awakens all our senses and alerts our minds and spirits. The person who prays, lives more attentively.

Pray and watch—that is only possible if we don't pray mystically with closed eyes, but pray messianically, with eyes open for God's future in the world. Christian faith is not blind faith. It is the wakeful expectation of God which touched all our senses. The early Christians prayed standing, looking up, with outstretched arms and wide-open eyes, ready to walk or to leap forward. We can see this from the pictures in the catacombs in Rome. Their posture reflects tense expectation, not quiet heart-searching. We don't watch just because of the dangers that threaten us. We are expecting the salvation of the world. We are watching in God's Advent. With tense attention, we open all our senses for the coming of God into our lives.

Watch and pray. It is the ancient wisdom of the masters of prayer and meditation that it is good to pray in the morning, at the dawn of the day, in the hour between sleeping and waking, and to rejoice in the reality of God and his world.

Concentrating; praying; waking up; watching and praying: all this reveals to our lives the daybreak colors of the future, and it leads to the call of Jesus, who, having watched and prayed in Gethsemane, called to his sleeping disciples: "Get up, let us be going."

"Watch and be sober" (1 Thess. 5:6, 8). That is the next thing we hear. If what we seek is boundless enthusiasm, this brings us down to earth. Those who are sober are the ones who are not drunk and so don't suffer from hallucinations, and don't let themselves be deluded by illusions, either pious or secular. When sobriety is added to the wakefulness that comes from praying, we shall neither fool ourselves nor let ourselves be fooled. We shall see reality as it is, and expose ourselves to it in its ordinary guise as well as in its surprises. Then we shall discover that reality is far more fantastic than our best fantasies. But we shall perceive too that the pain which reality imposes on us is better than the self-immunizations with which we try to protect ourselves, but through which we, in fact, barricade ourselves.

But in German the word for "sober" can also mean "empty"—an empty stomach. People who are "sober" in this sense have not yet eaten anything, and they begin the day fasting. They are hungry. In a transferred sense we call realists sober. They see reality as it is. If we are sober in this sense, *we are hungry for reality*, for God is in the reality; and then we forget the thousand possibilities we imagine. One single experienced reality is richer than a thousand conceived-of-possibilities. That is why contact with reality is so important.

The person who is sober and watchful is aware in good time of the impending dangers, and is not taken by surprise when their attack comes. He is aware of them, not just in private life but also in societal solidarity: "Be sober, be watchful, for your adversary the devil prowls about like a roaring lion, seeking someone to devour. Resist him, firm in your faith, knowing that the same suffering is endured by your brethren throughout the world" (1 Pet. 5:8, 9).

Watch and expect. When we wake up in the morning we expect the new day; and in the same way, the waking which springs from prayer to God also leads to the expectation of God in the life we experience. I wake up, and open all my senses for life, and for death too—for the fulfillments and also for the disappointments—for what is painful as well as for what gives joy. I expect the presence of God in everything I meet and everything I do. God's history with me, and with us, goes on. There is nothing more exhilarating than to experience this life-history with God in full awareness. What has God in mind for me? What does God expect of me? What is God saying to me through the things that are happening in the world?

Watch and see. Remarkably enough, watching and praying have nothing to do with faith, but everything to do with seeing. "The Lord opens the eyes of the blind" (Ps. 146:8); and Israel's Wisdom tells us even that "the hearing ear and the seeing eye are both made by the Lord" (Prov. 20:12). For it is by no means a matter of course that people who have eyes can also see, and that people with ears can hear. "Seeing, they do not see," complains Jesus, according to Matt. 13:13, and "hearing they hear not. They understand nothing." He means the presence of the kingdom of God among us. But he means his presence among us today, too: "I was hungry and you gave me no food, I was thirsty and you gave me no drink, I was a stranger and you did not welcome me." Then they will answer, "Lord, *when did we see you* hungry or thirsty or a stranger or sick?" Then he will answer them, "What you did to one of the least of these, you did (or did not do) to me." And that is the greatest judgment pronounced on us.

How do we learn to have seeing eyes for Christ's presence among us? Where are our eyes opened? Archbishop Oscar Arnulfo Romero was a faithful, conservative churchman. When he was fifty-nine years old he had a conversion experience. "He discovered in the poor the way of faith in God," writes Jon Sobrino. "In all the crucified men and women of history, the crucified God became present to him. . . . In the faces of the poor he saw the distorted face of God." Romero put himself on their side, and, a short time afterward, he was shot in front of the altar in the church in San Salvador, at the orders of the rich.

Where was God when the mass murders took place in the World Trade Center on September 11? Ought we to ask why God permitted this catastrophe, and answer like some well-known fundamentalist preachers: it was because God wanted to punish secular, liberal, or homosexual America? But wouldn't that mean that our God is the God of terrorists, and that the terrorists were the servants who carried out God's orders? Rather, ought we not to ask: *where was God* in those mass murders, and look for his presence among the victims? Doesn't God weep over the death of so many of his beloved children? Jesus wept over the coming destruction of Jerusalem (Luke 19:41). So tears will have run down the face of the suffering God at Ground Zero, and people who believe in God for Christ's sake are called to "stand beside God in his suffering," as Dietrich Bonhoeffer wrote during the resistance to the Nazi murderers.

Watch and perceive. To go through life with eyes open for God, to see Christ in oppressed and unimportant people—that is what praying and watching is all about. We believe so that we can see, not so that we can shut our eyes to the world. We believe so that we can see—and can endure what we see.

If we want to sum up what watching and praying is about, we have to say: it is about an attentive life. Goodwill and helpfulness are fine, but they are not enough. Attentiveness is necessary, so that we can do the right thing at the right time in the right place.

Live attentively: that means going into the new day, wholly present in mind, heart, and senses, in order to be present in that day with all our senses and all our powers, in the place where God is waiting for us.

"WATCHMAN, WHAT OF THE NIGHT?"

Darkness—night—is always a symbol for the God-forsakenness of the world and for the experience of being lost. In the darkness and in the night we see nothing, and the best thing is to sleep until day. There is an apt passage in Isaiah: in exile and far from home, strangers among strangers, the prisoners come to the prophet and ask: "Watchman, what of the night?" He answers: "The morning is coming but it is still night. If you will enquire, come back again" (Isa. 21:12). But Paul, Christ's witness, proclaims: "The night is far gone, the day is at hand let us then cast off the works of darkness and put on the armor of light" (Rom. 13:12). So it is "time to get up from sleep" and to live in the light of God's new day.

In these daybreak colors of Christ's day we will pray and watch, watch and be sober, watch and expect God, see and perceive Christ in our midst, and learn to live attentively in God's spirit, wholly present with all our senses and all our powers.

In our dreams, each of us is alone. But when we wake up we are in a world we share with others, for as Heraclitus said: "The wakeful share a world, whereas every sleeper turns to the world that is his alone." The wakeful perceive and know each other in the world they share.

"Get up," says Christ to the benumbed disciples, "and let us be going."

VII
TERROR AND THE CHRISTIAN FAITH
Leroy S. Rouner

On the morning of September 11, I went to the South Tamworth Country Store to get gas and the paper. The TV was on, as it always is, and I saw a large plane crash into a tall building. I thought it was an action film. My ten-year-old grandson would have said "Oh, cool!" Then a newscaster came on, and I realized it wasn't a movie. I called my wife and told her to turn on the TV, and that I'd be home in a minute.

Our youngest son, Jonathan, and our daughter, Christina, both live in Brooklyn. He is an investment banker with Credit-Suisse First Boston. His office is at their headquarters in midtown Manhattan, but the firm maintains a small office in the World Trade Center, so we called him first. His wife, Katrin, said that he had taken off from La-Guardia airport at 8:50 that morning on an American Airlines flight for Dallas. As the plane made its long, lazy turn to the west after takeoff he had seen smoke from lower Manhattan and wondered what it was. Later the pilot announced that they had to land in Detroit. Jonathan spent the next five days there before he could get home.

Christina is an actor and had the day off, so she walked over to be with Katrin and the children that afternoon. They live in the Cobble Hill section of Brooklyn, only a few miles from the World Trade Center. White ash had settled over Brooklyn after the attack, and everywhere there were pieces of paper with blackened edges and World Trade Center letterheads which had drifted over the river and were now stuck in the trees amid the bright fall foliage. Someone's work for that day. Christina saved some of them as a kind of tribute to the dead.

I live in a very small town at the edge of the north country of New Hampshire, which is a lot safer than New York. We don't lock our houses when we go to the store, and there aren't enough of us here to make it worth a suicide bombing. Still, in the deepest sense, it doesn't make any difference where you live. Everyone, everywhere, has a new sense of vulnerability, and the issue for us all is how we live with that—creatively, effectively, without being terrified.

How is it possible to walk with God without running scared? Where do we turn for equanimity in the face of terror's disruptions?

When Martin Luther was asked what he would do if he knew the world would end tomorrow he is said to have replied: "I would plant a tree today." Some dismiss that as Luther being cute, but I think he was on to something. That something is fundamentally different from the popular stoicism of our time, which gives solace to so many. That stoicism links the Romans and Hindus of old, and the psychiatrists, "spirituality" teachers, and Buddhist and New Age gurus of today, who say that if you can control your own inner feelings about your life, nothing external can really hurt you. For a people who hurt—and who among us has no spiritual pain?—this is a hopeful message.

The great hymn to this philosophy of life is Kipling's famous poem "If."

> If you can keep your head when all about you
> Are losing theirs, and blaming it on you.
> If you can trust yourself when all men doubt you,
> Yet make allowance for their doubting, too.

If you can make a pile of all your winnings,
And risk it on one game of pitch and toss,
And lose, and start again from your beginnings
And never breathe a word about your loss.
If you can walk with crowds and keep your virtue,
And talk with Kings, nor lose your common touch.
If neither foes nor loving friends can hurt you,
If all men count with you, but none too much.
If you can dream and not make dreams your master.
If you can think and not make thoughts your aim.
If you can meet with triumph and disaster
And treat those two imposters just the same.
If you can force your heart and nerve and sinew
To serve your turn long after they are gone,
And so hold on when there is nothing in you
Except the will that says to them, Hold On!
If you can fill the unforgiving minute
With sixty seconds worth of distance run,
Yours is the earth and everything that's in it,
And, what is more, you'll be a man, my son.

For all its nineteenth-century chauvinism of the British male stiff upper lip, there is something genuinely noble about this ideal. Every year I read this poem to my students in Indian philosophy as an illustration of the meeting place between the stolid stoicism of the British colonialists, and the exquisite stoicism of Indian nondualist philosophy and culture. Because I love dramatic readings, and because this is such a dramatic poem, both they and I are close to tears at the end. Surely we would all be glad for such spiritual poise and emotional equanimity. And just as surely, we all instinctively admire anyone whose character even approaches those qualities. So why isn't that what we should aspire to in coping with our newly discovered vulnerability? Why isn't this the way to walk in a fragile world?

There are two reasons.

One is simply that very few people have the inner moral strength to live that way. In the history of our philosophies of life, certain moral qualities and spiritual attitudes are much celebrated by generation after generation of sages, teachers, and philosophers who fail to notice that neither they nor practically anyone else can actually do that. There are, indeed, a few individuals who can, and they are the key to the second reason why this life option is morally unacceptable, because—for all its gracious expression of humane values—it is profoundly antihumanist.

My first glimmer of this antihumanism came in a history of Western philosophy class with John Herman Randall Jr. when I was in graduate school at Columbia. He was lecturing on the Roman Stoics, and he remarked that Stoic virtues were cultivated primarily to enhance the inner souls/ spirits/psyches of the Stoics themselves, rather than the lives of those to whom the virtues were directed. Hence, Randall noted, the Stoics were glad when their friends needed them, because it gave them an opportunity to practice the virtue of friendship and thus become better people themselves.

Stoicism—from the ancient Hindus to the present day—cherishes its "inwardness" as the pearl of great price. The message is: "Sacrifice anything necessary to maintain your equanimity; it is the only thing about your life that you can completely control. That control will keep you from being terrified and make you happy; and that is what we all want."

For those few who can live the life of Kipling's hero, I think that is true. What has not been noticed sufficiently, however, is the price to be paid for this equanimity. What the Harvard philosopher Ernest Hocking once called "the spiritual iron of the East" results from what both Hindus and Buddhists call "detachment."

Which takes us back to Kipling. How do you "meet with triumph and disaster, and treat those two imposters just the same"? You do it by not caring deeply about the triumphs and disasters in your actual, historical life. You detach yourself from criticism and applause. You live for the melding of your deepest identity with the divine Holy World Power, or some sort of ultimate reality, which is beyond the pettiness of "triumph and disaster" in ordinary life. You affirm your identity with that Power as something which lives underneath the discrepancies of a life divided among the supposed realities of space, time, and distinct personal identities. These all present themselves as ultimately valuable but they are, in fact, deceptive.

In this Indian view, our realistic, commonsense perception of life is a trick which the world has played on us. Hindu philosophy calls it *maya*, which means "illusion." Life in the world is a bad joke, which we must take in good humor and a spirit of kindly playfulness because it is what presents itself to us, and what we must therefore deal with. But freedom from pain—which is the primary goal of all stoicisms—means that we are not deceived by the "imposters" which surround us. *Moksha*, which means "freedom from pain," depends on our ability to "realize" or be "enlightened" about the trick that is being played on us.

This is even true if the issue concerns not those generalized and removed public occasions of politics, or policy, but the most intimate attachments of human life. What if it is a terrible personal loss, like the death of a child? Marcus Aurelius, the great sage of Roman Stoicism, is ready. He noted that the ordinary man prayed that his little son not be taken from him, but that the enlightened man prayed that when his little son was taken from him "let me not be disturbed." That is the antihumane price to be paid for the equanimity of this inwardness. The great sacrifice is love, because love cannot be detached, and it must suffer.

There is, of course, a Christian version of this anti-humanism. I heard it once from a very distinguished man who had lost a son. He gathered his family together, declaring that this was the will of God, and that they were to celebrate God's will more than they were to mourn their loss. My friend and co-author Bill Coffin had a different and deeper Christian response when he, too, lost a son who accidentally drove off a bridge into deep water and was drowned. When someone tried to comfort him with the affirmation that it was God's will, he said immediately that, when that car went in the water and his son drowned, the first heart to break was the heart of Almighty God.

Stoicisms, of whatever sort, are for the elite few, people of enormous spiritual strength. I don't know how they do it, and I don't want to make that sacrifice. To tell the truth, I'm one of those moral and spiritual travelers who knows himself to be weak, in spite of my strengths, and who yearns for a strong Savior to bless me and carry me along the way of this lovely and troubled life, and, in the end, to bring me safely home to the arms of a loving and forgiving God.

So most of us will never be able to walk with God in a fragile world unless we can bring our own fragilities with us. We know that we are unable to make ourselves less fragile, so we need the sure and certain hope that our fragilities will somehow be taken care of, so that we can get on with the business of being God's people and doing God's work in the world as we know it. Christian faith is the assurance that the world is not a bad joke. It is a world which God made, and pronounced good. More than that, it is a world in which God himself made His home. That is the message of the philosophically incoherent doctrine of the Trinity. Jesus, the

Christ, became God with us—not a Transcendental Ideal, but a living, personal presence in the midst of our history. So our world is God's world, and our work is the work God calls us to do in it. But we can't do that work if we are running scared. We need to be able to give that fragility, and all our other weaknesses, over to God. We need to confess our sins and be forgiven and sent on our way, rejoicing in the power and presence of God, and ready to do His work in the world. In order to do that, however, we need to understand the nature of the terror which afflicts us.

First of all, terror is destabilizing. The Stoics are right that we need equanimity in order to work creatively, and our reason can combine with spiritual maturity, recognizing that life has always been precarious. That understanding will provide a measure of equanimity. The fear of an attack, however, is specific. We know what we are afraid of, and we have some idea of how to prevent many types of attack. The insidious nature of our present situation, however, is that terrorism has touched on something deeper in us all which is pervasive, unspecific, and has no immediate remedy. It is that fundamental anxiety which is part of the human condition, the troubled sense that there is something incomplete, out of joint, or just plain bad in our lives, and we are not quite sure what it is.

When we, or others, do something wrong we often say, rather jauntily and by way of acceptance or excuse, "Well, nobody's perfect." True enough; but, what regularly goes unnoticed is that we are not very happy about that. Why do we have occasions when, for no particular reason, we wake in the night with the feeling that all is not well, and can't for the life of us say why we feel that way? We roll over and think, "I shouldn't have had that third Scotch-on-the-rocks" but somewhere in the far distance of our soul's reach we hear ironic laughter and the whispered words,

"Maybe so; but it's not the Scotch." Well, what is it? It is a brief insight into the human condition.

We are not who we most long to be. We are not "our true selves," whatever that means. We don't think about this often because we have cultivated denial. It is not that we are necessarily bad, although who among us is without moral regrets? It is that we know ourselves to be somehow incomplete, unfulfilled, and deeply in need.

This was what St. Augustine was thinking as he began his *Confessions* with the statement, "Lord, Thou has made us for Thyself; and our souls are restless 'till they find their rest in Thee." We are separated from that "true self" which is the "image of God" in us, because we are separated from God. The positive name for this dimension of self-awareness is nostalgia; the longing for home; the soul's journey back to one's true self, who is hid with Christ in God. The negative name for our malaise is original sin. The Stoics believe they can save themselves, so they do not walk with God in a fragile world, they walk with themselves in a world which they have made safe against pain. Christians know that God's world has always been fragile. God made it that way when He created human freedom and watched, wincing, while His children proceeded to walk their own way.

So what arms us against terror? How is it possible that—as the great hymn puts it—

> Through the night of doubt and sorrow
> Onward moves the pilgrim band
> Singing songs of expectation
> Marching to the Promised Land—?

That is what Christian faith is about. Faith is where weakness becomes strength because we are called out of ourselves to "be strong in the Lord." Faith is the conviction that, in the end, "all will be well, and all manner of thing be well." Faith celebrates St. Paul's persuasion in the eighth chapter of Romans, that "nothing in all creation can separate us from the love of God, which is in Christ Jesus, our Lord." Faith makes it possible for us to emulate Martin Luther, planting a tree with a glad heart—even though the world may be ending—in preparation for God's tomorrow.

Fragility and restlessness are inherent in the human condition. It is faith in God, not the noble courage of the Stoics, that enables our friendship with the future, and our deeds of love today.

VIII
THE SOLITUDE OF GOD
ELIE WIESEL

Solitude: does there exist for man, for the creator, for a Jew, a problem more laden with anxiety? At once crushing and necessary, solitude both defines and denies; what would I be without it, what would become of me if there were nothing else on my horizon? Created in God's image, man is as alone as He is. And yet: man may and must hope; he must rise to the challenge, transcend himself until he loses—or finds himself. Only God is condemned to eternal loneliness. Only God is truly, irreducibly alone.

The Hasidic and mystical Masters are obsessed by the subject. For them, God is often to be pitied. Yes, indeed, God inspires not only love and piety, justice, and charity but also compassion and pity. To be more precise: in opening his heart and his soul to the troubling and exalting mysteries of creation, man cannot but feel pity, in the purest sense of the word, for the Creator. Pity for the Father who suffers with His children who suffer—often at His hands—pity for the weary Judge wounded by his own severity; pity for the King whose crown is so often dragged through the dust, whose Word is misheard, misunderstood, misinterpreted; pity for the Lord who is everywhere, at all times, in every thought, in everything, in every deed, even in pain, even in evil, even in want, even in absence that rends human beings, prisoners one of the other and each one imprisoned in his loneliness.

For what would man be were he not, at the core, a living appeal hurled toward his fellowman to break his own solitude? Let him succeed completely, and he will be diminished: he would know from the start that he cannot follow it to the end, worse, that he must not follow it to the end?

Adam, solitary, has no problem: and therein lies his problem. "It is not good for Man to live alone," decrees God. And Adam discovers Eve, his companion, at his side. Is she his problem? No, he himself is the problem when he comes face-to-face with Eve. Before, he found his solitude heavy; now, he misses it. Before, he did not know he was alone; only now has he discovered it. From now on, he will live in a vicious circle: the less alone he is because there is someone living with him, the more aware he is of his loneliness. The solution? There is none. There cannot be.

This is why solitude is the basis of so many philosophical quests and so many religious movements. I say "I," without knowing to what or rather to whom I refer. Every reflective process starts out with an indispensable division of the self. "I say to myself this or that": Who am I? The one who speaks or the one who listens? The two forms of the I, the two I's, are separated by a wall which only an absolute and immortal conscience would be able to scale. On both sides of the wall, the "I" lives alone. And yet, each is rooted in the loneliness of the other. That is why a certain Jewish traditions forbids the use of the singular "I," only God may say "I," *Anokhi*, only God may define Himself as "I." For He never needs to transcend Himself.

But enough of this meditation. No matter which way it goes, it always leads us back to ourselves.

When I was a child, living in a small Jewish town nestled in the Carpathian Mountains, I dreaded solitude. Left alone, I felt abandoned. At night I would eagerly wait up for my teachers and schoolmates to arrive. What if something had happened to them? More than anything else, I feared finding myself alone, cut off, excluded from their experiences, even the bad ones. I knew, in some obscure way, that if I had a chance of survival, it was by clinging to my family, to my community. To live or survive outside seemed to me inconceivable. In other words: I could accept collective but not individual solitude.

Collective solitude did not frighten me; I was used to it. It has been our lot since Egypt, since Sinai. It is inherent in our condition: to wish to be different is to isolate oneself. Living in a pagan and idolatrous society, we were for a time alone in believing in one God, alone in accepting His Law, alone in remaining faithful to Him. In a violent world, we were alone in opposing murder, falsehood, debauchery, slavery, and, above all, humiliation, the worst form of slavery. At that stage, however, isolation did not mean the exclusion of others, and certainly not the denial of others. We believed, in accordance with Jewish tradition, that the Torah, the essence of Judaism, was good for the Jews, that it helped us keep alive our identity. In other words: by following his own path, by strengthening his identification with the Torah, the Jew is able to fulfill himself under the sign of the truth; and, likewise, a non-Jew can, by following *his* path, attain the same degree of truth. Each aspires to universality, and each can attain it by using his or her individuality as a starting point. To be a Jew meant—and means—to be and live not in opposition to others, but beside others. The pagan prophet Bileam meant to curse us by calling isolation upon us; strangely, his curse turned into a blessing. In time, it again became a curse. But by then, the phrase *levadad yishkon* had come to signify not isolation but exclusion.

This exclusion prevailed on all levels: exclusion from society, from history, and finally, from humanity. To wit: the ghettos, the deprivations, the pogroms, the heinous and absurd accusations, the racial and religious persecutions throughout the centuries and throughout all the lands of Christendom, the altars of Nazism called Auschwitz and Treblinka. Of what did my ancestors and their descendants die if not of the fact that humanity had decided to exclude them, the better to trample, mutilate, and annihilate them?

The procedure was simple and efficient. They took our virtues, distorted them until we were stereotypes and caricatures. Then they blamed us for our customs, our caricature-like ways of handling our religion and our lives. They turned our choice to be different into a desire for exclusivity, our solitude into isolation, our loyalty into servitude, our faith into despair.

There are times when I'm not sure which is more astonishing: the solitude imposed upon us from outside or our stubborn efforts to break through it—without, however, yielding at the core, that is, with regard to those elements that constitute its substance and its strength.

Our methods were many and varied: we devoted ourselves to study not only so as to acquire a knowledge of the past but also to become acquainted with our precursors. Because of them, thanks to them, we felt less alone. Herein lies the secret and the power of Talmud: its characters have remained alive, have remained present. They challenged us just as if they were our contemporaries, as if our problems were theirs and theirs were ours. I am Rabbi Shimon bar Yohai in his cave and he is less alone, so am I; I listen to Rabbi Akiba and his voice touches me, as the voice of Rabbi Zeira stirs me. Their present is not my past—it is my own present.

If the Hasidic movement has won such rapid victories, if in the eighteenth century it succeeded within just a few years in taking root in so many Jewish communities from the Dnieper River to the Carpathian Mountains, it is because it offered an answer to, and perhaps even a cure for, loneliness.

A Hasid is never alone: even when he is, he has his Rabbi, his Master, with him, within him; he need only evoke his Sabbath face to shatter the loneliness. If life weighs too heavily upon him, if he feels discouraged, depressed, he need only tear himself away from his everyday existence and present himself at the Rabbi's court. And there, he is sure to meet friends and companions, rich and poor, learned and not-so-learned. And together they will affirm their belief that, for better or worse, man has received not only the dubious gift of hearing the most implacable loneliness but also the ability to overcome it, to transform it into hope and yearning. In later years I never again felt anything like the joy and happiness I knew as a child and adolescent, when I was with our Hasidim and our Master, whether on Shabbat or some special holiday. Even today, after all those years, I often feel overcome by nostalgia for those encounters, for that joy, for that sense of fulfillment. No loneliness, no suffering, could prevail against them.

I remember, I remember some of the Hasidim over there, in the kingdom of Night. There, we knew the ultimate edge of all experience, for there we crossed the boundaries of anguish, of solitude, and of the battle against them. Anguish beyond anguish, solitude within solitude, naked despair, sadness stripped of all disguise, of all speech, and of all semblance of civilization: that is what their universe was made of. Many—some of the best—almost succumbed. Fathers and sons suddenly became enemies over a crust of bread. Friends and brothers tore each other to pieces for a spoonful of soup, a moment of respite, a warmer vest. If you knew the number of liberal intellectuals among the Kapos, the number of sadists among the intellectuals! Well, yes, that is how it was: there were many who made the wrong choice. Forgetting all the principles of their upbringing, they failed when it came to the test. But there were those who clung to their faith, such as the priests who resisted, and it gave them the strength to hold up: not one of them agreed to collaborate in order to save his skin. And the same is true, and even more so, of the rabbis: not one—I repeat, not one—agreed to accept the little scrap of power offered him which would have enabled him to live—or live better, or a bit longer—at the expense of his comrades in misfortune. On the contrary, they showed a selflessness that left the killers perplexed. As for the Hasidim, who are the subject of this meditation, they rose higher than the heavens aided by their faith and by their solidarity: their communal prayers on the Days of the New Year, their determination to celebrate with joy—yes, you heard me correctly, with joy—the Festival of the Law. And all this in a place where, as he sought to dehumanize his victim, the killer succeeded only in dehumanizing himself. Even today, my reason fails to grasp the hidden meaning, the brutal truth of what I witnessed: the two sides of humanity—one so pure, the other so base—how could it happen? How could anyone pray to God at Birkenau, in the shadow of the ovens—how was it possible? How could we invoke God on the very ruins of His creation?

These are the themes I deal with in my tales. In other words, they haunt even my writing. A teller of tales, I too try to shape solitude into a weapon against solitude.

To write—what does that mean? I take words which belong to everybody. I take them—and make them mine; they bear my signature and my seal. Each one reflects me, condemns me, or remains faithful to me. Between the words I use and myself, the link becomes charged: I am alone with them, but I would be more alone without them.

Sooner or later, they become my reason for living and for working. Whence their ambivalence: when they sing, I feel exalted; when they are gray and humdrum, I feel diminished.

Every creative person knows these peaks of ambition and depths of depression. Samuel Beckett writes *en desespoir de cause*s (in desperation). Rabbi Nahman told stories to make them into prayers.

If another could write my tales, I would not have written them for I have written them to give evidence. I see my role as that of witness. Which explains the loneliness that weighs on every one of my sentences, on every one of my silences. Each book is at once my first and my last. And each tale relates the life and struggle of the first and the last Jew, who share each other's solitude. Not to tell, or to tell something else, would be to betray them, to abandon them, and worse: to bear false witness. When I evoke Sighet or Jerusalem, Abraham or the Baal Shem Tov, my purpose is to make them into my allies in communicating with my contemporaries.

And what about during the long days of darkness—did our ancestors sustain us then? Our loneliness in those years was unmatched. Abandoned by mankind, forgotten by God, the Jew felt discarded by Creation. There came a moment of total despair and, in a way, it was. It was the end of an era, the end of an illusion. Perhaps even the end of the world—except that it takes time for the realization to sink in. Orwell was not only a writer—he was in his own way a prophet. Is it by chance that he pinpointed the year 1984 as a turning point? I think not. We need only sink further into complacency and let ourselves forget, and assuredly the fallout of Auschwitz will trigger the Hiroshima of tomorrow.

But, you will ask me, what about the Messiah? I believe in him still. I believe in him with all my heart, more than before. But his coming depends on us. As it is said in the Kabbalah: the coming of the Redeemer, the how and the when, will be determined by man, not by the Lord.

Which brings me back to the beginning, to my proposition which speaks of pity: pity for God.

Certainly, like everybody, I have known anger and I have raised my voice in protest. I do not regret it. But, over the years, I have come to understand the double-edged nature of the questioning that modern man endures: even as I have the right to ask the Judge of all men, "Why did you allow Auschwitz to happen?" so has He the right to ask us, "Why have you made a mess of my creation? By what right have you cut down the trees of life and made of them an altar to death?" And all of a sudden you think of God, in His heavenly and luminous loneliness, and you feel like weeping. For Him and over Him. And you weep so much that He too—so many Talmudic traditions—He too begins to weep, until your tears and His come together and merge like two melancholy solitudes, thirsting for fulfillment.

IX

WHERE IN THE (POSTMODERN) WORLD IS GOD?

JEREMY LANGFORD

A NEW WORLD (DIS)ORDER

Flipping through the newspaper on a February morning before work, an image and caption stopped me cold: "Nobel Prize winner Leon Lederman moves the Bulletin of Atomic Scientists' Doomsday Clock ahead to 11:53 at the University of Chicago." The accompanying article went on to quote Lederman, a 1988 Nobel Prize–winning physicist, as saying that the scientists who first worked on nuclear reactions in the 1940s never dreamed of the "incredible overkill" that the United States and Soviet Union put into weapons of mass destruction. "I doubt that they could ever imagine that we could do anything that absurd," he said. The board of the *Bulletin* stated that they were moving the clock's hands to reflect their "growing concern that the international community has hit the 'snooze' button rather than respond to the alarm" of nuclear disaster.

The absurdity of it all turned my morning ritual into one of lamentation as the image in the paper ran through my mind: an elderly scientist moving the hands of a huge clock that, instead of keeping time, marks the end of time brought about by human hands. Unable to focus on any of the manuscripts on Scripture, social justice, and the Catholic tradition sitting on my desk, an existential crisis of spirit overcame me. As I stared out my window watching the Chicago "El" train whisk people off to their jobs downtown, I wondered when we became disconnected from our Source, from the earth, from each other? When did it become okay to walk past one another anonymously? When did we decide splitting an atom was grounds for splitting faith and reason, might from right, strong from weak, God from would-be gods? Just as I had done so many times over the years, I flipped through the limp piles of paper containing words of exegetical wisdom, of hard-won faith, of pleas for social justice and love, and they seemed so irrelevant. Do these words and the world they represent speak to the contemporary culture? Can they really point to an all-powerful, all-loving God in the face of so much violence and destruction? Are they powerful enough to increase faith and lead to world harmony? Why publish them at all? How did I end up in Catholic publishing in the first place?

Growing up I had a strong sense that the world was in disarray. Some of my earliest memories include the Watergate scandal and subsequent impeachment proceedings of President Richard M. Nixon as well as public debates about whether to pull U.S. troops out of Vietnam. The assassinations of John Kennedy, Martin Luther King Jr., and Bobby Kennedy as well as the horrible rioting and police action at the 1968 Democratic National Convention in Chicago loomed in the background.

All the while my peers and I faced divorce in many more ways than the dissolution of marriages and the breakdown of the family, making us what I call *Generation eX*. Throughout the sixties, seventies, and eighties America underwent a series of divorces that injured or dissolved the bond between the past and the present; institutions and those they were supposed to serve; companies and their employees; education systems and their students; federal structures such as welfare, social security, and both the taxpayers who fund them and the beneficiaries intended to receive them. Among other cuts, government spending on financial aid for disadvantaged families was dramatically reduced, leaving many families without the food stamps, school lunch programs, health care assistance, and federal housing help they had come to rely on. In 1974, Generation eX earned the dubious title of being the most impoverished generation in post-Depression America as we experienced the escalation of many negative forces such as child abductions, nuclear threat, drug and alcohol use, teenage sex and pregnancies, anorexia, AIDS, cynicism, and suicide. As we entered high school, budgets were being cut and schools were literally and figuratively falling apart. At the same time the cost of college was soaring, the job market was shrinking, the cost of homes was rising, and the institutions of health care and social security were ailing.

The modern era's dream of a golden age of technology-based prosperity, reason in human conduct, an end to war, and remarkable advancement of all humankind had turned into the nightmare of the bloodiest century in history. In place of these things capitalism and consumerism took hold like never before. Like so many in my generation, I spent countless hours in front of the television watching MTV, playing video games, listening to music, buying into the latest fads, and culling meaning from the popular culture. One of the most popular fads of the day was the Swatch watch, and I owned at least three. Little did I realize that Swatch watches were a shining symbol of our culture's obsession with time, technology, and consumerism. As slogans like "time is money" and "shop till you drop" became more and more popular, so did the need for counter-slogans encouraging families and friends to spend more "quality time" with each other. The faster the world moved, the more people, and God, seemed to get left behind in the whirlwind. There was a feeling that nothing really mattered anyway, so why not indulge?

Yet, I often wondered, now that we can do more in less time, are we really better off? Unlike our agrarian ancestors and the monks who invented the bell tower to help them pray regularly, we feel unraveled and inefficient without our day planners—which offer us inspiring quotes, lessons in prioritizing, and never-ending columns for our to-do lists. But are we really more balanced because we can jam more into our days? We feel lost without our watches, which not only record hundredths of seconds but also gauge our heart rates, miles walked, and direction we are going. But are we any more at home in the world with mini navigational systems on our arms? We feel isolated without our cell phones, which now report the news, track stock quotes, and send and receive e-mail. But are we really any more connected to other people when we talk to them from our cars?

Today we live in what is being described as *postmodern* culture in which the modern categories of time, space, and order are playfully subverted. Postmodern shopping malls and hotels, for example, reverse natural order and put the outside inside—the latter even contains the former—as fountains, trees, and "outdoor cafés" coexist with stores in ideal human-made climates. Clocks rarely appear in such public spaces, as the distinction between night and day is blurred and time seems endless or frozen. Nothing looks old or worn, as age is the enemy. And the mind is lulled into an alter-world in which marketing is the message and spending becomes easier the more it is disconnected from the realities of budgets and bank accounts. Computers, portable CD players, and home theater systems create virtual realities that have no boundaries of time, space, or order. Microwave ovens allow people to cook "food" faster than ever, reducing meal preparation and consumption to a matter of mere practical function. Fax machines and e-mail collapse time and depersonalize communication. The globalized economy ensures that a McDonald's will be on every street corner and that the long arm of Hollywood will shape values in countries where subtitles are no longer needed as English continues to become the international language. Worldwide CNN brings the countless battlefields into our living rooms and makes global terrorism both a reality as well as a virtual reality. For example, as I sat in front of my television on the morning of September 11, 2001, packing for a trip to New York the following day, I literally could not believe the scene being played out before me— my mind flashed back and forth between clips of the movie *Independence Day* and the reality of people running from the crumbling World Trade Center towers.

In the postmodern world that I have known most of my life, the self-assured rationalistic outlook of a Western-style modernism has been supplanted by a skepticism of ordered progress toward a defined goal (who defines the goal or sets the plan to reach that goal in the first place?); a global culture in which the powerful use and even deplete the resources of weaker countries in the name of capitalism, and different belief systems meet face-to-face and call into question universalized Truth and metanarratives; a belief that is tenuous at best; and an acceptance of pluralism, relativism, and deconstructionism that rejects metaphysical or religious signs and symbols that remain static rather than transmorphing with the times. Increasingly people know more but expect less and are polarized into different camps on issues of morality, truth, education, culture. In many cases the generation gap widens as previous generations either know or are hotly in pursuit of the "real thing" while younger people place enormous weight on freedom mixed with subjective experience and find a myriad of real things, or, as Bono of U2 sings about, those things that are "even better than the real thing." And the melting-pot America that the modern mind so desperately sought is instead a microcosm of a globalized world in which the "other" of different cultures, educations, religions, political and ethnic traditions, and sexual orientations demands to be heard and not appropriated.

SEEKING THE GOD WHO SEEKS US

Unlike in the modern era, the question today is not so much about proving God's existence as it is about experiencing God's existence. Theologians range from, those who argue for a premodern understanding of God that exempts all talk of God from contemporary scientific and intellectual scrutiny to those who embrace the pluralism and diversity of the day to the point of not talking about God at all. Somewhere in between, theologians put God in conversation with the culture without baptizing the culture or compromising revelation or tradition.

I fall into this middle road.

All my life I have struggled to reconcile faith in God with the world I see and experience. For reasons that belong to the realm of mystery, the moments of clarity, in which God's presence is obvious to me, come and go. Like a cosmic game of hide-and-go-seek, now I see God, now I don't. Sometimes I find God right where I figured I would—in long conversations with close friends, at the dinner table with family, in hugs from loved ones, at weddings, funerals, and baptisms. Other times I am surprised to find God, as Catholic novelist Flannery O'Connor once wrote, "flitting from tree to tree in the back of our minds," calling me to look more deeply into who I am, daring me to drop my baggage and run free. And sometimes God finds me just when I least expect it, when I have turned my back and given up.

None of us can describe God, exactly, but we know when we have God moments. We know it in our souls. They are moments of recognition when we know what is true, realize what is real, and experience what is good. God moments are rare glimpses into eternity that happen in time. They are moments pregnant with love and life that help us give birth to our best selves and encourage others to find their best selves. They are moments that fill us with thanksgiving, overwhelm us with joy, offer us hope, and transforms a moment in time (*chronos*) into a sacred moment (*chairos*) that fuels our journey. They are moments that teach us that faith really matters, that the stories of God's creation and ongoing love always exist, even if we put them on the cutting room floor in a world of soundbites and shattered meaning.

The trouble with God moments is that we forget them so easily. We go right back to playing hide-and-go-seek with God. Sometimes God hides and we find her. Sometimes we hide and he finds us. But the eternal question: "Where in the world is God?" echoes in the marrow of our bones.

Growing up in the seventies, especially in the post–Vatican II Catholic tradition, catechesis and faith formation backed off the premodern conception of God as the eschatological grounding of all being in favor of one that people could dig at all times: God is love. The joke among my peers is that our sense of Catholic religious education back then was, "Hey, man, God is love, now go draw a rainbow." I remember being very glad that God loved me, but I had no idea what God was like, what God's love was like, or what I was supposed to do with God's love.

I remember wondering where God was when my parents got divorced, if God really wanted an annulment so either or both of them could remarry, and if God's love was as fragile as human love. My parents were always sincere in their desire for my brother and me to have faith and to ask questions. Religion was never jammed down our throats. Instead, it was always there, even in pale shades, for us to see as a vehicle for love, community, social action—especially in the midst of the messiness of life. There was a clear sense that the Catholic tradition is beautiful while not being perfect.

After attending Catholic junior high school, which was a good experience and education, I went to a big public high school. It was not long before whatever relationship I had with God fizzled. In some ways it felt good to question and rebel against God along with everything else at that age. I see now that God was on my mind a lot—various journals I kept are loaded with questions about the meaning of life, our purpose here, how it all began, why love is so painful at times, and where in the world God might be.

I had a pretty good idea that I could find God in the churches I knew as a kid. The church building was God's "house" on earth, and the Roman Catholic Church was the second in command to God as head of the household. But somewhere along the way I got to thinking that God had too many houses to be in them all at the same time. And if he could be in them all simultaneously, then I wondered why would God limit himself to just Catholic churches? Why wouldn't he fill every space that groaned with emptiness or claimed to be his home? And, by that logic, why would he confine himself to one religion or to bricks and mortar—why wouldn't God just set himself loose in the world? My response was to view religion and church in a constricting way—human-made rules of moral rigidity that don't take into account the human condition, statues of saints peering down in plastered perfection, threats of hell, a spirituality of guilt. No thank you.

I entered my freshman year at Notre Dame skeptical that I would find God and suspicious of anyone who had found God. But my defensive walls were quickly surmounted by thoughtful peers, many of whom came from Catholic prep schools and knew much more about Catholicism than I did, but who were seekers like me; classes that integrated church teaching with modern questions and problems; and a dorm life that included chapel, prayer, communion and community, spiritual growth and social outreach opportunities that became more and more appealing as I worked to understand who I was, who God is, and what this life is all about. I went on to study English literature and philosophy because their starting point was experience and love of knowledge, but I used many of my electives dabbling in theology, trying to reconcile the experience of God with intellectual commentary on that experience. My curriculum was safe—it allowed me to be a seeker poking at God without being overly bound by a church I perceived as being authoritarian to the point of preferring a blind believer over one struggling to see with the eyes of faith.

Seeing with the eyes of faith became very difficult for me once I graduated and moved to Chicago. Though I had a job as an editor at a Catholic publishing house, my work life was in many ways an intellectual exercise more than a faith-shaping experience, a coveted job for a liberal arts major. On the streets of the city, I encountered, for the first time, homelessness, drug deals, crime, racism, and the anonymous hustle and bustle of the workaday world. And I felt very alone and helpless. The God I had known in the safe environment of college was nowhere to be found in the city. I rarely if ever had conversations with people about their faith. The few churches I checked out were not as welcoming as the dorm chapel, and the sermons were disconnected from my life. Besides, my studio apartment was too small to accommodate God anyway! So I walked out into the world alone.

While I was quite satisfied to call myself "spiritual but not religious," what never left me was my Catholic sensibility to seek God in all things and to see the world itself as a sacrament that tells us of God and God's love. In the secular city it seemed that seeking God was naive. But once I looked underneath the secular posturing of the city, or at least my perception of it, I realized that the quest for meaning—for something more, for the sacred, for God—was all around me. At work I tracked the growing sales of books on religion and spirituality and saw that, perhaps in the wake of the modern mind-set, people were again seeking the sacred, wishing for enchantment, hungry for meaning. In coffee shops and on public transportation I overheard people talking about work, life, family, meaning, God. Suddenly it hit me that we are all joined together by our seeking. And then I finally realized that the Christian tradition embraces seekers. Jesus himself remains one of the most passionate seekers of all time. And in seeking peace and justice, love and mercy, healing and reconciliation, Jesus laid the foundation for the New Testament and the Christian tradition.

When I doubt my convictions or forget that Jesus and Christianity embrace seekers, I turn to the Bible to remind myself that I am not alone in asking questions and that, no matter what, I am loved. For these reasons, one of my favorite Bible stories is John 1:35–38 in which Jesus asks two curious men following him, "What do you seek?" and invites them to "Come and See." In those few words Jesus asks the great question and extends the great invitation of Christianity. By asking, "What do you seek?" Jesus is also asking,

"Who are you?" "Where are you going?" "How will you get there?" The great promise of Christianity is that in asking we receive, in knocking we gain entrance, and in seeking we find. The religious rub here is that in holding Christianity to its promise, we are held to asking questions, thinking about why we are here, celebrating the solidarity of all creation, loving and forgiving others, working for peace and justice. These are not actions only for religious people. They are for anyone seeking to live more deeply.

To help us live more deeply, Jesus invites us to come and see. Seeing with the eyes of faith is never easy—Jesus' own disciples struggled mightily and, even after seeing all he had shown them, did not know what to make of the empty tomb and did not recognize the resurrected Jesus until he gave them a sign. In today's fast-paced world, we squint to make sense of the blurs streaming past our faces. Meaning changes, eluding our grasp. Knowledge is revised and supplanted by yet more knowledge. Truths come and go. Gurus and self-proclaimed prophets have their moments and fade into the distance. But, as with the dejected disciples on the road to Emmaus, Jesus walks with us until we have eyes to see and ears to hear. Throughout his ministry, Jesus healed those who lived physically and metaphorically in the darkness. But he did more than help them see in a human way; he shared his light with them so that they could see who he was and who they could become. Time and again Jesus shows us that believing and seeing are paths to each other— seeing leads to believing, but, more importantly in this age, believing leads to seeing. He also shows us that seeing with the eyes of faith is often a gradual process and that, when we come to see with the eyes of faith, the only proof of what we see is the way we live and love.

For me, finding a church with an active faith community and rooting my spiritual quest in religion has made all the difference. While I do not believe in a God hermetically sealed off from the world or a Church more concerned with its own survival as an institution than with the God it points toward, I also do not believe in a God fashioned by the culture or a church that does not rely on tradition and revelation to speak its message. I take very seriously the notion that the church is a pilgrim church feeling its way forward as a collective body of the people of God who work to proclaim the Good News, serve those in need, and bring fulfillment and love to the world.

In this postmodern, fragile world walking with God is not easy. Universal truths no longer exist, so we retreat to what we think we can know by empirical evidence or direct experience. We occupy our minds and time with material possessions and worldly pursuits. We even anesthetize ourselves with alcohol and drugs. We simply cannot bear the thought of standing as we are, naked before ourselves, the world, or God.

Our biblical ancestors Adam and Eve knew this feeling. After they had eaten the fruit from the forbidden tree of knowledge, they "heard the sound of the Lord God walking in the garden at the time of the evening breeze, and the man and his wife hid themselves from the presence of the Lord God among the trees of the garden." God seeks them out calling, "Where are you?" to which Adam responds, "I heard the sound of you in the garden, and I was afraid, because I was naked" (Gen. 3:8–14). I wonder how I would react if I heard God walking toward me in the cool of the evening. Would I, like Adam and Eve, run and hide because I have clothed myself in knowledge of the day and separated myself from God. Would I feel ashamed at being naked before a God who knows me not by my résumé or possessions but by my very soul?

Jesus himself knew what it was like to be stripped naked before his friends, enemies, family, and God. After he was crucified, the soldiers divided his clothes into four parts and cast lots for his tunic, which was "seamless, woven in one piece from the top" (John 19:22–24).

I have often wished I could clothe myself in the seamless garment of faith. But I cannot. And so I pray, in this fragmented age, that I might stitch together enough fragments of faith to know God's love and be an instrument of it. In truth, I am grateful for being stitches away from losing faith, from being naked and alone, because it reminds me of my fragility and my solidarity with all those who are fragile. And it is in my most fragile moments when I turn to God and to others and walk in faith, hope, and love in this fragile world.

Part Three

PAST THE GATES OF HELL

"there comes a time when one must look away from death and turn away from the dead; one must cling to life, which is made of minutes, not necessarily years, and surely not centuries; one must fight so as not to be overwhelmed by history but to act upon it concretely, simply, humanly. In the midst of national catastrophe, one must continue to teach and study, bake and sell bread, plant trees and count on the future. One must not wait for the tragedy to end before building or rebuilding; one must do it in the very face of tragedy."

—Elie Wiesel, *Five Biblical Portraits*

X
SEEING THINGS AS THEY REALLY ARE
Karen Armstrong

September 11, 2001, was a revelation in the original sense of the word. It was an "unveiling," which laid bare a reality that had been there all the time, but which we had not seen with sufficient clarity. The atrocities showed us the extreme precariousness of our position in a world in which the vast majority of the population feel dispossessed and hopeless. During the weeks leading up to September 11, the main news story in Britain had been the asylum seekers, who try to break into the United Kingdom with a desperation matched only by their tenacity. Every night some eighty to ninety refugees attempt to walk through the Channel Tunnel; others cling to the undercarriage of trains. Long-distance drivers open their trucks and find them full of people. Our ports are now crawling with police and sniffer-dogs. In fact, England was beginning to seem like a privileged, gated community in the midst of a dangerous city. As I watched the Twin Towers fall on that terrible day, I found myself thinking of these refugees. Like it or not, we now live in one world; we cannot continue to exist in our bubble of privilege. If we try to shut the world out or retreat from its problems—as the Bush administration had intended—the world will come to us, in desperate or in fearful ways.

We cannot go back to the security that we thought we had enjoyed on September 10 because it was an illusion. Religion is often seen as a panacea, which enables us to look at the world through rose-tinted spectacles. But only low-grade religion does this; true faith is not an emotional security blanket nor does it take away the pain that is an inescapable part of the human condition. It demands that we perceive things as they really are. If we cannot be clear-eyed about the things we see, we have no hope of glimpsing a reality that is present but unseen. Our whole vision will be skewed. I am currently researching a book about the Axial Age [800–200 B.C.E.], the period when all the great religions which have continued to nourish humanity came into being: Confucianism and Taoism in China; Hinduism, Jainism, and Buddhism in the Indian subcontinent; monotheism in the Middle East; and rationalism in Greece. This is not simply an exercise in spiritual archaeology; the sages who pioneered these great traditions have rarely been surpassed, and they have a great deal to teach us in our current predicament. They often challenge the way we practice our religion today, because it sometimes seems to me that we frequently reproduce exactly the kind of attitudes that such people as the Buddha, Isaiah, or Socrates were trying to get rid of.

One of the great lessons of the Axial Age is that we must see things clearly, "as they really are." This is a phrase that constantly recurs. Before an aspirant could even begin to practise yoga, for example, he or she had to undergo a strict moral regimen, which included the obligation to speak the truth at all times. Until this was second nature, a budding Buddhist or Jain could not undertake the simplest yogic exercise. Speaking the truth is quite a rare accomplishment; we often embellish, exaggerate, soften, or otherwise distort the information we are trying to convey. We hide from unwelcome facts, which seem too hard to bear or which put us in an unflattering light. But unless we look at reality clearly and see it as it truly is, we cannot begin our spiritual quest.

In the same way, the prophets of Israel did not put a positive, comforting gloss on the disastrous political crises of the Middle East in their day. They told their people in no uncertain terms that the kingdoms of Israel and Judah were going to be destroyed by the powerful new empires of Assyria and Babylon. Nor did they assume that God would automatically be on the side of his people, as he had been at the time of the exodus from Egypt. Isaiah and Jeremiah called the people who preached a more consoling and hopeful message "false prophets." Instead of nurturing these delusive dreams, they counseled the people of Israel to brace up, see the situation as it really was, and examine their own behavior. The prophets were not gloomy defeatists. They were right: first Israel and then Judah really were annihilated, Jerusalem reduced to rubble and the Temple destroyed.

Before September 11, we thought we were safe, but then we watched the symbols of the economic and military power of the United States, which we had assumed would ensure our security, crumble like a house of cards before the wrath of the "other" world. Now, like the ancient people of Israel before us, we too must see things as they are. Our world *is* fragile; it always has been so, but we did not see this until the veil had been stripped away from a truth that should have been staring us in the face. If we can bring ourselves to see the reality of our situation, we will become healthier in mind and heart.

Indeed, if we respond creatively to this tragedy, we could be on the brink of a new spiritual adventure. Religion was implicated in the September atrocities and this should be a warning to us. Like any human activity, religion can be abused, and this is what can happen if the fear and pain that lie at the heart of every single fundamentalist movement that I have studied in Judaism, Christianity, or Islam festers and goes sour. Our suffering can harden us and make us distort the very traditions that we are attempting to defend. We need a spiritual revolution in the West, and the fearful new conditions of our lives provide exactly the right environment for such a venture.

The people of the Axial Age, too, were living in a violent and terrifying world. All the people who developed one of these new ideologies were caught up in one devastating war after another, which threatened to overthrow civilization. All the great sages and prophets gazed steadily at this fearful spectacle and struggled to find a new solution. The Bhagavad Gita, one of the holiest scriptures of the Hindu tradition, is actually set on the battlefield; and it is there, on the front line, that Prince Arjuna is commanded to work out his salvation. But violence and terror were the context that made this spiritual revolution a possibility. Later, Christianity and Islam—latter-day statements of Axial Age monotheism—also made this journey from warfare to peace. And now, since September 11, we in the First World are living on the front line. Our world has become a battlefield, and it is here that we have to find our salvation, too.

We cannot avoid suffering, and, unless we fully realize this, we cannot even begin our spiritual quest. The Buddha made this clear in the First Noble Truth of his spiritual method. "Existence," he said, "is *dukkha*" (Vinaya Mahavagga 1:6; Samyutta Nikaya 56:11), a word often translated to mean "suffering," but which is more accurately rendered as "unsatisfactory, awry." Even when we are apparently happy, there is usually something amiss. When we achieve something we had longed for, we may find that it is not in fact what we really wanted. Or we immediately start to worry about losing it. Or else our happiness depends upon the deprivation of somebody else. I became acutely aware of this a couple of months before September 11, when I watched a television documentary about Indonesia. Our politicians have praised this country as an economic miracle, but this program showed that, while a small elite had indeed made a lot of money, most of the people were caught in an appalling poverty trap. The cameras took us inside a factory where men and women were making jeans and shirts for Western companies working thirty-six hour shifts for a dollar a day. As I watched, I found myself repeating the Buddha's maxim. There truly was something awry about our Western comfort and security.

There is a mythical story about the Buddha, which shows how important it is to understand the ubiquity of suffering (Jataka 1:54–65). It is said that when little Sidhatta Gotama was five days old, his father gave a great feast to which he invited the local priests to examine the baby's body, according to their special lore, and tell his fortune. One of these priests predicted that the little boy would one day see four very disturbing sights: he would see an old man, a sick man, a corpse, and a monk. This would convince him to renounce the world and become a wandering ascetic. Eventually he would become a Buddha, an enlightened human being who would assuage the pain of humanity. The future Buddha's father was not happy about this because he had envisaged a more worldly career for his son, so he carefully shielded the child from the spectacle of any suffering whatsoever. Sidhatta was brought up in a palace, surrounded by a pleasure park; guards were posted at each gate to prevent any suffering person breaking through to the young man.

Sidhatta's father is exactly the kind of authority figure that Buddhism would reject, because this tradition insists that everybody must be responsible for his or her own life-decisions, and must never depend in this way upon anybody else. And the pleasure park is a striking image of the human mind in denial. It is always tempting to shut out the suffering that surrounds us on all sides, and pretend that it has nothing to do with us. But this is futile because, despite our best efforts, suffering will always break in, obliterating the cautionary barricades we erect around ourselves. And so it proved with Sidhatta. When he was twenty-nine years old, the gods—who knew his destiny—decided that he had lived in this fool's paradise long enough. They sent four of their number disguised as an old man, a sick man, a corpse, and a monk into the park. They were able to evade the guards, and the spectacle so shocked the future Buddha that he immediately resolved to leave home that very night and become an ascetic.

This is an exemplary tale, designed to show an aspirant what he or she must do to attain enlightenment. If we remain in a deluded state, blocking out the pain that is an inescapable part of the human condition, we remain trapped in an infantile, and inauthentic, version of ourselves. Because we are not seeing things as they truly are, we cannot attain true illumination. But when Sidhatta allowed suffering to invade his world and his whole being, he was ready to begin his quest. This awakening is painful; it tore his life apart, and Sidhatta had to be prepared to leave his old self behind. This is always frightening because it means that we have to abandon the only way that we know how to live. The effort of bringing a new self to birth will entail long and hard labor. But if we manage it, our lives—and the lives of everybody around us—are immeasurably enriched.

All the great world traditions put suffering right at the top of the agenda. For Jews, the image has traditionally been the state of exile—of the displacement, dislocation, and loneliness which not only afflicts all thinking human beings but, the mystics suggest, even the Godhead itself. This is not dissimilar to the *hijrah,* or "migration," that

Muslims envisage as the prelude to new spiritual insight, the same painful connotations of uprooting and severance from a beloved and familiar lifestyle. Christians have the image of the crucified Christ, reminding them that new life can only come after we have been torn apart. Now suffering has broken into the United States; Americans have been attacked on their own soil. Life can never be the same again. And, though it is sad and frightening to leave that old, secure lifestyle behind, it is an opportunity that could lead to great things.

In his classic book *The Idea of the Holy*, Rudolf Otto described the experience of what we call God as *mysterium terrible et fascinans*. It is a mystery that is fascinating and enticing because we recognize it at a profound level; it is within ourselves, at the ground of our own being. But it also fills us with dread. We need only think of Isaiah in the Temple, who cried out that he was lost and near to death when he saw a vision of his God (Isa. 6:3). Jeremiah experienced the divine as a pain that wracked his every limb and which made him stagger around like a drunk (Jer. 23:9; Jer. 20:7, 9). When Ezekiel had his vision of the divine chariot, he was literally knocked out by it, and lay on his bed like one stunned for seven whole days (Ezek. 2:15). God is sometimes experienced as a devastating shock that shatters all our preconceptions. Otto describes this numinous experience as one of dependency, since we suddenly realize our extreme frailty and vulnerability. Since September 11, we can all relate to this in a wholly new way. Hindus might tell us that God exists beyond good and evil; and that the terrible destruction we saw on that day was a revelation of the divine. We might not be ready for that insight yet. But we can draw upon our new insecurity and fear as a preparation for a deeper experience of the Sacred.

This is because egotism and pride hold us back from enlightenment. All the greatest spiritual masters tell us this. The Koran calls this attitude *istaqa*, that is, "self-sufficiency" (Koran 96:6–8). People think that they can save themselves, that their great wealth will protect them; they do not need Allah, because they can manage their own lives and do it all by themselves (Koran 104:1–3). They will get a shock on the Last Day, when the divine reality will break through this hard carapace of pride (Koran 70:11–14). The word *kafir* is usually translated "unbeliever," but it really means "one who is ungrateful to God." Such a person knows that God is the Creator and all-powerful but claims that his achievements are all his own. The first thing that Muhammad made his converts do was to prostrate themselves in prayer several times a day. It was hard for the Arabs, who did not believe in kingship, to grovel on the ground like a slave, but the posture of their bodies was designed to teach them, at a level deeper than the purely rational, what is required when we make a surrender (Islam) of our whole lives to God. We have to abandon the posturing, preening ego if the divine is to become a reality in our lives. This is probably what Jesus meant when he said that to enter the Kingdom of Heaven we must become like little children.

In the West, we deliberately cultivate an attitude of independence. This can, of course, be extremely positive, but not if this independence is allowed to harden into an unrealistic pride and selfishness. St. Paul quotes a very early Christian hymn which speaks of the *kenosis* or "self-emptying" of Jesus, who did not cling to his dignity as a man made in God's image, but accepted the condition of a servant and became wholly obedient (Phil. 2:6–11). This is the attitude that Muslims call *Islam*, and they see it reflected in the life of the prophet Muhammad. But in all three of the monotheistic traditions, people have also imagined a similar *kenosis* within God himself.

Thus the great sixteenth-century Kabbalist Isaac Luria evolved a new creation myth, which was immediately taken up by Jews all over the world because it reflected the terrifying world in which they lived far more than the orderly account in the first chapter of Genesis. In 1492, the Christians had expelled the Jews from Spain, where for centuries they had lived peaceably and fruitfully under Muslim rule. Jews mourned the loss of Spain as the greatest catastrophe to have befallen their people since the destruction of their Temple by the Romans in 70 C.E. In the rest of Europe too, Jews were cast out of one city, one region after another. Luria's new creation myth is a violent, wrenching process, punctuated by explosions, mistakes, and false starts, which begins by God acting ruthlessly toward himself. Because God is everywhere, there is no room for the world. So to make a space for the world to come into being, God, as it were, vacates a region of himself in an act of *tsimtsum*, "withdrawal." He makes himself less, deliberately diminishes himself in order that our world may come into being.

Christians imagined a *kenosis* in the heart of the Trinity. Christianity imagines the Father pouring himself out entirely into the Son. He transmits all that he *is* to the Son, giving up everything—even the possibility of expressing himself in another Word. Once that Word has been spoken, as it were, the Father remains silent; there is nothing more that we can say about him, since the only God we know is the Logos, the Son. The Father, therefore, has no identity, no "I" in the normal sense, and confounds our notion of personality.

The Greek Orthodox speak of the "ecstasy" of God, a word that literally means "to stand outside the self" that takes him beyond himself to the fragile realm of created being. As the great fifth-century theologian, who used the pseudonym Denys the Areopagite, explains:

> And we must dare to affirm [for it is the truth] that the Creator of the universe himself, in his beautiful and good yearning towards the universe . . . is transported outside himself in his providential activities towards allthings that have being . . . and so is drawn from his transcendent throne above all things to dwell within the heart of all things, through an ecstatic power that is above being and whereby he yet stays within himself (*The Divine Names* 4:3).

In the classical Greek tradition, Aristotle had seen God as utterly remote from humanity, involved only in the delighted contemplation of himself. But for Denys, God had given up this transcendent isolation, which made him aloof to the transient concerns of this world, and had entered our world of pain and flux. Denys saw this ecstasy as required of every Christian. This was the hidden or esoteric message of the Bible and it was reflected in the smallest gestures of the liturgy. Thus when the celebrant leaves the altar at the beginning of the Mass to walk through the congregation, sprinkling the people with holy water before returning to the sanctuary, he is imitating the divine ecstasy, whereby God abandons his isolation and merges himself with his creatures.

Muslims too imagined a God who could suffer. Some believed that the Arabic noun *ilah* [god] sprang from the etymological root *WLH*: "to be sad, to sigh for." There was a sacred tradition, which imagined God saying: "I was a hidden treasure and I yearned to be known. Then I created creatures in order to be known by them." There was no rational proof for this divine sadness, of course, but God is the supreme archetype. We are created in his image, so that when we humans experience sorrow or yearn for something to fulfill our deepest desires, when we weep over the tragedy of life, this must reflect God. Our grief must mirror a sympathy with the pathos of God himself. The immensely influential thirteenth-century mystic Muid ad-Din ibn al-Arabi imagined the solitary God sighing with longing before the Creation. But this sigh was not an expression of maudlin self-pity. It had an active creative force, which brought the whole of our cosmos into existence. It also exhaled human beings, who became *logoi*, "words" that express God to himself. It follows that each human being is a unique epiphany of the hidden God, manifesting him in a particular and unrepeatable manner.

These are, of course, great myths, sacred fictions that express an important and fundamental truth. These mystics knew, from their own experience, that we are most fully ourselves when we give ourselves away. Therefore this must, in some sense, reflect a reality in God, too. They depict God as abandoning his lofty self-sufficiency and voluntarily walking with us in a fragile world. If we want to be where God is, therefore, it is no use clinging to proud, isolationist policies or to the self-assertion of belligerent patriotism. That is not where God is to be found. We have a better chance of a numinous experience in our new vulnerability, which God himself, somehow, shares. These myths also tell us that God in some sense gave himself up in the act of creation; we too know that when we are egotistic and selfish we are at our least creative. A work of art that screams "Me! Me! Me!" is unlikely to be much good. These myths have a special relevance for us at this perilous juncture of history, when we need to be more creative than ever before if we are to find a solution to the world's ills.

The ecstasy of God as described by Denys, like the creative sigh of Allah in Iban al-Arabi's myth, is inspired by compassion. God felt pity for the uncreated beings who would never know him; he wanted to share their pain. In all the great traditions of the Axial Age, compassion is the key. The sages and prophets recoiled from the violence of their times, and insisted that there was one infallible test of true spirituality. Every religious doctrine, every spiritual practice must issue in practical compassion or it is worthless. Confucius preached *jen* or "human-heartedness"; and, long before Rabbi Hillel or Jesus taught the Golden Rule: "Do not do unto others as you would not have done unto you" (Analects 12:2). In the Indian subcontinent, the sages were inspired by such tender-heartedness for all living beings that they practiced the ethic of *ahimsa* ("harmlessness") and would, if possible, avoid treading on an ant or a blade of grass in order to spare them pain. The Buddha taught his monks and lay followers alike a meditation that he called "the Immeasurables," because love could know no limit. They had to emit waves of benevolence to the four corners of the earth, not omitting a single creature from this radius of goodwill. The Prophets of Israel spoke of the prime duty of justice: care for the orphans, the widows, the strangers, and the oppressed, which was far more important than a decorous liturgy. The New Testament, like the Koran, is also full of this insight.

This is why the experience of suffering is so productive. If we do not suffer or feel that we should really be immune from suffering, it is all too easy to dismiss the pain of others. Once suffering has invaded our own lives, we can empathize more fully with the tragedies that afflict other people. Americans have joined the ranks of victims: they now have new insight into the fear, sorrow, and pain endured by the peoples of Rwanda, the Middle East, and

Bosnia. Our traditions all teach us that suffering must not imprison us in self-regard, but must be a springboard to an appreciation of the pain of others. Thus, Jewish Law commands: "If a stranger lives with you in your land, do not molest him. . . . You must count him as one of your countrymen and love him as yourself—*for you yourselves were once strangers in Egypt*" (Lev. 19:33–34). The memory of exile and slavery in Egypt cannot be a license to inflict further pain but an inspiration to compassion, the ability to "suffer with" others.

But compassion is not simply an ethical test; it is the means whereby we encounter the God who has chosen to walk in our fragile world. The Buddha insisted that the practice of compassion would bring a person *ceto vimutti,* the "release of the mind," which, in the Buddhist scriptures, is a synonym for the supreme Enlightenment of Nirvana. Those who practiced the "Immeasurables" would experience an "ecstasy" because they would transcend their selfishness and discover an enhanced existence, finding that they were imbued with "abundant, exalted, measureless loving-kindness." They would be taken right out of themselves: "above, below, around and everywhere," going beyond their usual limited point of view (Anguttara Nikaya 3:65).

Jesus also made the point that it was those who practiced compassion to the hungry, the sick, and the deprived who would enter the Kingdom of Heaven, the presence of God. If we really practiced the Golden Rule preached by Confucius, Rabbi Hillel, or Jesus (Shabbat 31a; Matt. 7:12) we would continually dethrone ourselves from the center of our universe and put another there. We would live in a state of ecstasy, in Denys's sense. Each time we were tempted to say something unkind about another person, another race, or another nation, but asked ourselves how we would like to hear ourselves spoken of in this way, and then refrained, we would momentarily have transcended that selfish impulse which makes us denigrate others in order to defend or promote ourselves. Sages and prophets do not preach the virtue of compassion because it sounds good; religious people are very pragmatic. All the great world faiths emphasize the importance of charity and loving-kindness because they work; they have been found to introduce us into a sacred realm of peace within ourselves. And they do that because they help us to transcend the demands of our insecure, greedy egotism that imprison us within our worst selves.

St. Paul shows us how the practice of compassion deflates the ego. In his famous hymn to charity he explains: "Love is always patient and kind; it is never jealous; love is never boastful or conceited; it is never rude or selfish; it does not take offense; and is not resentful. Love takes no pleasure in other people's sins, but delights in the truth; it is always ready to excuse, to trust, to hope, and to endure whatever comes" (1 Cor. 13:4–6). True religion has little to do with self-righteousness, which is often simply a self-congratulatory form of egotism. The discipline of compassion is the safest way to lay aside the selfishness and greed that hold us back from God and from our best selves.

These are desperate times and the world seems a dangerous place. But for the vast majority of human beings, who are not fortunate enough to live in the First World, it has always been desperate and dangerous. Very few could dream of the security and power symbolized by the towers of the World Trade Center. Now we have joined the dispossessed, but instead of resenting this, we can see it as an opportunity to effect the spiritual revolution which alone can save our troubled world.

XI

SEPTEMBER 11, 2001: A PACIFIST RESPONSE
Stanley Hauerwas

I want to write honestly about September 11, 2001. But it is not easy. Even now, some months after that horrible event, I find it hard to know what can be said or, perhaps more difficult, what should be said. Even more difficult, I am not sure for what or how I should pray. I am a Christian. I am a Christian pacifist. Being Christian and being a pacifist are not two things for me. I would not be a pacifist if I were not a Christian, and I find it hard to understand how one can be a Christian without being a pacifist. But what does a pacifist have to say in the face of terror? Pray for peace? I have no use for sentimentality.

Indeed, some have suggested pacifists have nothing to say in a time like the time after September 11, 2001. For example, the editors of the magazine *First Things* (December 2001) assert: "Those who in principle oppose the use of military force have no legitimate part in the discussion about how military force should be used." They do so because, according to them, the only form of pacifism that is defensible requires the disavowal by the pacifist of any political relevance. That is not the kind of pacifism I represent. I am a pacifist because I think nonviolence is the necessary condition for a politics not based on death. A politics that is not determined by the fear of death means no strong distinction can be drawn between politics and military force.

Yet, I cannot deny that September 11 creates and requires a kind of silence. We desperately want to "explain" what happened. Explanation domesticates terror, making it part of "our" world. I believe attempts to explain must be resisted. Rather, we should learn to wait before what we know not, hoping to gain time and place sufficient to learn how to speak without lying. I should like to think pacifism names the habits and community necessary to gain the time and place that is an alternative to revenge. But I do not pretend that I know how that is accomplished.

Part of the problem may be that I am such a neophyte pacifist. I never really wanted to be a pacifist. I am from rough people who survived by being rough. I had learned from Reinhold Niebuhr that if you desire justice you had better be ready to kill someone along the way. But then John Howard Yoder and his extraordinary book *The Politics of Jesus* came along. Yoder convinced me that if there is anything to this Christian "stuff," it must surely involve the conviction that the Son would rather die on the cross than for the world to be redeemed by violence. Moreover, the defeat of death through resurrection makes possible as well as necessary that Christians live nonviolently in a world of violence. Christian nonviolence is not a strategy to rid the world of violence. In short, Christians are not nonviolent because we believe our nonviolence is a strategy to rid the world of war, but, rather, because faithful followers of Christ in a world of war cannot imagine being anything else than nonviolent.

But what does a pacifist have to say in the face of the terror of September 11? I vaguely knew when I first declared I was a pacifist that it might have some serious consequences. To be nonviolent might even change my life. But I do not really think I understood what that change might entail until September 11. For example, after I declared I was a pacifist, I quit singing the "Star-Spangled Banner." I will stand when it is sung, particularly at baseball games, but I do not sing. Not to sing the "Star-Spangled Banner" is a small thing which reminds me that my first loyalty is not to the United States but to God and God's church. I confess it never crossed my mind that such small acts might, over the years, make my response to September 11 quite different from that of the good people who sing "God Bless America"—so different that I am left in saddened silence.

That difference, moreover, haunts me. My father was a bricklayer and a good American. He worked hard all his life and hoped his work would not only support his family but also make some contribution to our common life. He held a job critical to the war effort in World War II, so he was never drafted. Only one of his five bricklaying brothers was in that war, but he was never exposed to combat. My family was never militarized, but even as Texans they were good Americans. For most of my life I too was a good American, assuming that I owed much to the society that enabled me, the son of a bricklayer, to gain a Ph.D. at Yale— even if the Ph.D. was in theology.

Of course there was Vietnam. For many of us Vietnam was extended training necessary for the development of a more critical attitude toward the government of the United States. Yet, most of us critical of the war in Vietnam did not think our opposition to that war made us less loyal Americans. Indeed, the criticisms of the war were based on appeal to the highest American ideals. Vietnam was a time of great tension, but the politics of the antiwar movement did not require those opposed to the war to think of themselves as fundamentally standing outside the American mainstream. Most critics of Vietnam (just as many who now criticize the war in Afghanistan) based their dissent on their adherence to American ideals, which they felt the war was betraying. That is why I feel so isolated even among the critics of the war in Afghanistan. I do not even share their allegiance to American ideals.

Nor do I share the reaction of most Americans to the destruction of the World Trade Center. Of course I recoil from murder on such a scale, but I hope I remember that one murder is too many. I remain awe-struck by the collapse of those elegant buildings that at once appalled and attracted my attention. For I cannot deny I have a grudging respect for the sheer audacity of the attack as well as for the strange beauty in the image of the planes' graceful flight into those great towers. I am haunted by the terror those trapped in those buildings must have felt in recognizing that there was no escape. I admire the everyday courage of the police and the firemen who died doing their jobs. I am a pacifist, but a commitment to nonviolence makes me no less human.

However, I cannot now consider flying the flag in response to such an event. I have not flown the flag for thirty years. I even remove the one that some well-wishing person insists putting from time to time on my mailbox on the Fourth of July. The idea that I might put a flag pin in my lapel never crosses my mind. The only lapel pin I have ever worn is a small plowshare made from the melted down aluminum of a jet used by the American air force in Korea. A Roman Catholic layman in Des Moines, who is a pacifist, bought the jet as scrap with the intention of turning our modern swords into plowshares. Now that small and insignificant pin reminds me of how alien I have become (just desserts for someone who wrote a book entitled *Resident Aliens*).

Many of the people with whom I attend church do wear flags in their lapels or, if they are women, more decorative flag pins on their dresses. They are good and decent people. They have led lives of small and great sacrifice that put my own life to shame. They are very much like my parents, good Americans. They are patriots. In contrast I am not even sure what it means to claim my American citizenship. I have a friend, a Will Campbell "no bullshit" kind of Christian, who recently told me he no longer thinks of himself as an American, as a citizen. He lives and teaches in central Tennessee, but he refuses to acknowledge that living in Tennessee implies he must be loyal to that abstraction, America. Though I do not live in central Tennessee, I share his views. This at the very least means I am a conscientious objector in George Bush's war on terrorism.

But where does that leave me? Does it mean, as an estranged friend recently wrote me, that I disdain all "natural loyalties" that bind us together as human beings, even submitting such loyalties to a harsh and unforgiving standard? Does it mean that I speak as a solitary individual, failing to acknowledge that our lives are interwoven with the lives of others, those who have gone before, those among whom we live, those with whom we identify, and those with whom we are in communion? Do I forsake all forms of patriotism, failing to acknowledge that we as a people are better off because of the sacrifices that were made in World War II? To this I can only answer, "Yes." If you call patriotism "natural," I certainly do disavow that connection. Such a disavowal, I hope, does not mean I am unattentive to the gifts I have received from past and present neighbors.

In response to my friend, I pointed out that because he too is a Christian I assumed he also disdained some "natural loyalties." After all he had his children baptized. The "natural love" between parents and children is surely reconfigured when children are baptized into the death and resurrection of Christ. Saint Paul says:

> Do you know that all of us who have been baptized into Christ were baptized into his death? Therefore we have been buried with him by baptism into

death, so that, just as Christ was raised form the dead by the glory of the Father, so we too might walk in the newness of life. For if we have been united with him in a death like his, we will certainly be united with him in a resurrection like his (Rom. 6: 3–5).

Christians often tend to focus on being united with Christ in his resurrection, thereby forgetting that we are also united with him in his death. What could that mean if it does not mean that Christians must be ready to die, indeed have their children die, rather than betray the Gospel? Any love not transformed by the love of God cannot help but be the source of the violence we perpetrate on one another in the name of justice. Such a love may appear harsh and dreadful from the perspective of the world, but Christians believe such a love is life giving, not life denying.

Of course, living a life of nonviolence may be harsh. Certainly you have to imagine, and perhaps even face, that you will have to watch the innocent die for your convictions. But those who do so are no different from those who claim they would fight a just war. After all, the just warrior is committed to avoiding any direct attack on noncombatants, which might well mean that more people will die because the just warrior refuses to do an evil deed that good may come of it. For example, on just war grounds the bombings of Hiroshima and Nagasaki were clearly murder. If you are serious about just war, you must be ready to say that it would be better that more people died on the beaches of Japan than to have committed one murder, much less the bombing of civilian populations.

This last observation may suggest that, when all is said and done, a pacifist response to September 11 is just one more version of the anti-American sentiments expressed by what many consider to be the American Left. I say "what many consider" because it is very unclear if there is a Left that is left in America. Nowhere is that more apparent than in the support for the war on terrorism given by those who identify themselves as the "Left." Yet, although much has been made by some of the injustice of American foreign policy, the problem with such lines of criticism is that, no matter how immoral the American government's actions may have been in the world, such immorality cannot explain or justify the attack on the World Trade Center.

American imperialism, often celebrated as the new globalism, is a frightening power. It is frightening not only because of the harm such power inflicts on the innocent but because it is difficult to imagine alternatives. For example, pacifists are often challenged after an event like September 11 with the question: "Well, what alternative do you have to bombing Afghanistan?" Such questions assume that pacifists must have an alternative foreign policy. My only response is I do not have a foreign policy. I have something better—a church constituted by people who would rather die than kill.

Death is at the heart of the challenge presented by September 11. On that day, Americans were confronted by people ready to die as an expression of their profound moral commitments. Some say they chose death because they were desperate or, at least, represented a people who are in such desperate situations that death is preferable to life. Yet their willingness to die stands in stark contrast to a political establishment that asks the members of its community, in response to September 11, to go out and shop. It may be unfair to focus on this desperate attempt to reclaim "normalcy," but it surely is the case that nothing is quite as revealing about the character of American life than the capitalist ability to exploit patriotism for profit.

Ian Buruma and Vishai Margalit observe in an article entitled "Occidentalism"(*New York Review of Books*, January

17, 2002, 4–7) that lack of heroism is the hallmark of bourgeois ethos. Heroes court death. The bourgeois is addicted to personal safety. They concede that much in an affluent, market-driven society is mediocre, "but when contempt for bourgeois creature comforts becomes contempt for life itself you know the West is under attack." According to Buruma and Margalit, the West (which they point out is not just the geographical West) should oppose the full force of calculating antibourgeois heroism, of which al-Qaeda is but one representative, through the means we know best—for example, by cutting off their money supply. Of course, Buruma and Margalit do not tell us how that can be done, given the need for oil to sustain the bourgeois society they favor.

Christians are not called to be heroes. We are called to be holy. We do not think holiness is an individual achievement, but rather a set of practices to sustain a people who refuse to have their lives determined by the fear and denial of death. We believe that, by so living, we offer our non-Christian brothers and sisters an alternative to all politics based on the denial of death. Christians are acutely aware that we seldom are faithful to the gifts God has given us, but we hope the confession of our sins is a sign of hope in a world without hope. This means pacifists do have a response to September 11. Our response is to continue living in a manner that witnesses to our belief that the world was not changed on September 11. The world was changed during the celebration of a Passover in 33 C.E.

Mark and Louise Zwick, founders of the Houston Catholic Worker House of Hospitality, embody the life made possible by the death and resurrection of Jesus. They know, moreover, that Christian nonviolence cannot and must not be understood as a position that is no more than being "against violence." If pacifism is no more than "not violence," it betrays the form of life to which Christians believe they have been called by Christ. Drawing on Nicholas Berdyaev, the Zwicks rightly observe that "the split between the Gospel and our culture is the drama of our times," but they also remind us that "one does not free persons by detaching them from the bonds that paralyze them: one frees persons by attaching them to their destiny." Christian nonviolence is but another name for the friendship we believe God has made possible and constitutes the alternative to the violence that grips our lives.

I began by noting that I am not sure for what I should pray. But prayer often is a form of silence. The following prayer I hope does not drown out silence. I wrote the prayer as a devotion to begin a Duke Divinity School general meeting. I was able to write the prayer because of a short article I had just read in the *Houston Catholic Worker* (November 16, 2001) by Jean Vanier. Vanier is the founder of the La Arche movement—a movement that believes God has saved us by giving us the good work of living with and learning to be friends with those the world calls "retarded." I end with this prayer because it is all I have to give.

> Great God of surprise, our lives continue to be
> haunted by the spectra of September 11, 2001.
> Life must go on and we go on keeping on–even
> meeting again as the Divinity School Council.
> Is this what Barth meant in 1933 when
> he said we must go on "as though
> nothing has happened?"
> To go on as though nothing has happened can
> sound like a counsel of despair, of helplessness,
> of hopelessness.
> We want to act, to do something to reclaim the way
> things were.
> Which, I guess, is but a reminder that one of the
> reasons we are so shocked, so violated, by

9/11 is the challenge presented to our prideful
presumption that we are in control, that we are
going to get out of life alive.
To go on "as though nothing has happened" surely
requires us to acknowledge you are God and we
are not.
It is hard to remember that Jesus did not
come to make us safe, but rather he came
to make us disciples, citizens of your new
age, a kingdom of surprise.
That we live in the end times is surely the basis for
our conviction that you have given us all the time
we need to respond to 9/11 with "small
acts of beauty and tenderness," which Jean Vanier
tells us, if done with humility that we may
remember that the work we do today, the work we
do everyday, is false and pretentious if it fails to
serve those who day
in and day out are your small gestures of beauty
and tenderness.

XII
SAVING THE FLESH
Kathleen McManus, O.P.

It is not too much to say that in this moment of history everything is given over into our human hands. Truly, we hold in our hands life and death, hope and despair, the future—or the end of life as we know it. The tragedy of September 11, 2001, has, in what is now common parlance, "changed the world forever." Indeed, it has riveted the world's attention and reconfigured the ground upon which Americans stand. On that ground, our anguished efforts to regain a lost foothold have been expressed, by turns, in trembling knees, arrogant posturing, noble gestures of compassion, and many bold strides outward into a world newly threatening and threatened. Our need for a foothold initially led to excessive investment in the authority of the U.S. government, President Bush, and, ultimately, the U.S. military. Americans by and large were seized with desire to maintain and increase the comforting illusion of power in a world where good and evil were suddenly clearly delineated, and where our power could only advance the good. Our power promised salvation, not only for us but also for the rest of the world.

The ground reconfigured by September 11 thus shifted the symbol of authority to centerfield. At the same time, America's unbridled war against terrorism quickly evoked resistance, at least in some quarters, to the ways authority was exercised at home and in Afghanistan. The tragedy that made us know our own vulnerability had not prevented us from inflicting harm on a people already vulnerable, poor, and afraid.

The symbol of authority that equated itself with power was not, after all, saving the world. The question arose: is the dominant symbol of authority as power saving anyone? Is it saving those in whose name it is wielded? Is it even saving those who wield it? And, if it isn't, then what sort of power, what sort of authority, really saves?

Even as the symbol of authority is thus both sought after and questioned, a cataclysm of events internationally in the political arena and domestically in both the corporate and the religious spheres has contributed to the disintegration of trust, the escalation of fear, and a universally heightened sense of the fragility of flesh. A resurgence of violence between Israel and Palestine has evoked horror at atrocities perpetrated by both sides as well as a diminishing ability to trust the leaders of either nation. U.S. diplomatic interventions, motivated more by political self-interest than genuine justice seeking, have failed to yield results. Political and economic crises suffered by so many Latin American nations evoke superficial attention, but never the concern for truth that might lead us to reflect upon our own role in the affliction of our neighbors. And, in our own country, the moral impact of corporate corruption at Enron pales in light of evidence that certain members of the Roman Catholic hierarchy have systematically covered up victims' allegations of childhood sexual abuse by members of the clergy. In a world "changed forever," none of these issues of religious moral authority can remain isolated news items. Issues of international and domestic politics and issues of religious moral authority are palpably interwoven now as never before; indeed, they are interwoven in the fabric of even my individual life. As a native New Yorker now living in Oregon, as a Blauvelt Dominican sister in a worldwide order of preachers founded in the thirteenth century in the service of Truth, as one who has ministered among Latinos in the Bronx and is now engaged as a theologian in poignant dialogue with my Latin American counterparts, indeed, as a woman religious who has long struggled with the exclusively male authority structure of the Roman Catholic Church, I experience the dilemmas of our age in the particularities of my own existence and through the network of relationships and institutions to which my own choices have committed me.

NEW YORK IN OREGON; THE UNITED STATES IN LATIN AMERICA

In the wake of September 11, even from across the country, I shared New York's desire to draw protective walls around a city and nation stunned by a new and disconcerting vulnerability. Sisters and associates of my Dominican community and neighbors of my childhood lost loved ones in the attack; my brother lost former colleagues in the NYPD. And at the University of Portland where I teach, our women's soccer team shared the grief of a teammate whose mother died on the Boston–Los Angeles plane that plunged into the towers. She was on her way to watch her daughter's team play. Everywhere I turned, even here on the distant West Coast, the attack was personal.

While the attack was pervasively personal, however, the experience of victimization was far from one-dimensional. My students, confused and shaken, were hungry for accompaniment in reflecting upon the meaning of the tragedy. Their reflections occupied a continuum from forceful patriotism to probing analysis of the sources of terrorism. While some delivered a trenchant critique of U.S. global policies, other struggled painfully to come to grips with why so many people hate America. And then there were our Muslim students who experienced double jeopardy: they shared America's grief, but they deplored the perception that their beloved Islamic faith could be the source of such horror. I will never forget Mansour, a passionately devout Muslim from Saudi Arabia who sought me out to check on the welfare of my family in New York. So conflicted was he that he offered an emotional apology simply because other Arabs were responsible for the tragedy. Yes, the attack was pervasively personal, but victimization was experienced on multiple fronts.

Scarcely more than two weeks after September 11, I made my way to Lima, Peru, for a long-planned inter-American conference on women and globalization. Dominican women theologians from across Latin America gathered with six North Americans to engage in social analysis and theological reflection upon the sufferings and the oppression experienced by people in our diverse societies who are the victims of a globalized economy. While our Latin American sisters expressed compassion for us in the wake of our tragedy, their eyes communicated the sad awareness that the tragic violence marking ordinary reality for their people had, quite simply, quite inevitably, come home to disturb the comfort of the giant to the north. They were appalled by the terrorist attacks, but they were all too familiar with the desperate impoverishment grounding such acts. And on October 7, as the United States began its bombing of perhaps the poorest nation on earth, these Latin American women embraced us, their culpable, horrified North American sisters, in a circle of tears. Women in solidarity across boundaries of culture, race, economic class, and national politics. Women committed to proclaim truth in a darkened world. Where was there a symbol of truth in the reality so variously perceived by that world?

The diverse scenarios depicted above merely suggest the chaos and complexity of the world we live in, a world that, since September 11, seems more than ever to seek some symbol of authentic authority by which to gauge what is true and trustworthy amid so much internal and external darkness and destruction. The symbol we seek may be right before our eyes; it may be hidden in the one image that has captivated the world more than any other since September 11. The symbol of the real power that may yet save us emerges in the ever-present image of Ground Zero.

A SYMBOL OF AUTHORITY?

Easter 2002 dawned upon workers still struggling to uncover bodies from the tomb beneath what was once the World Trade Center. As the gruesome task that began on September 11 neared its end, firefighters, police, and ironworkers traversed the dark, airless caverns of twisted steel many levels below the ground. This was the last, most perilous leg of a devastating journey of exploration. Cutting through metal beams, reinforcing crumbling underground walls against the waters of New York harbor, these workers knew that their risk of joining the victims grew with each passing hour. But this was not the fear that imbued their task with urgency. Their urgency was fueled by a different fear, and that was the fear that work at the site would officially come to a close before they had succeeded in recovering the victims' remains.

Saving flesh. Recovering traces of humanity from the pit of destruction. Amid the diverse responses to September 11, this focus on the flesh of the victims has been a constant at the site of the tragedy in New York. How can this image serve as a focus of meaning for the rest of the world? How can deep reflection upon this image facilitate the emergence of life from the tomb? Indeed, how might Ground Zero function as the symbol of authority that so many cry out for?

EXCAVATING THE SYMBOL

The rubble of the World Trade Center's Twin Towers in New York marks what has become, and will ever be, holy ground. Ceaseless pilgrimages and countless mementos placed by mourners witness to lives lost and futures forever altered by what occurred on the site. What once seemed an impenetrable mountain of debris has, through months of arduous labor, been reduced to "The Pit." The sacredness the Pit has acquired in imaginations all over the world testifies to its efficacy as a real symbol of the sort of power that saves. The key to unlock this symbol lies in the questions we ask of it, questions that enable us to articulate and thereby release the power concealed in the tragic image of Ground Zero.

What is it, precisely, in this gruesome image that has so captivated us? What emotions has it called forth, and what do these emotions reveal about our humanity? How has the emotional response to this image created bonds among disparate persons, bonds transcending differences of faith, class, ethnicity, transcending even opposing ideologies? What is the nature of those bonds, and what do they reveal about us? What are the implications of the religious tone of the language evoked by Ground Zero? How are we to interpret the frequency of public religious expression and the increased yearning for spirituality in our society in the wake of September 11? Finally, is it too much to say that what has been encountered in the depths of this symbol of our own vulnerability is, in fact, God?

The right questions lead us to the conditions of hope hidden in Ground Zero. Indeed, the force that captivates us indicates not only the conditions but also the living presence of hope at the very site of destruction. Our search for answers begins with an examination of the activities and events characteristic of life for those engaged in the recovery effort.

LIFE AT GROUND ZERO

The numbing shock inflicted on September 11 has gradually been absorbed and transmuted by a variety of personnel doing the long-term, multifaceted work of recovery. Initially, the desperate efforts of firefighters, police, and other rescue workers were focused on finding survivors. Soon, the futility of this effort became grievously apparent, and the focus shifted to recovering the remains of victims. Stories of valor witness to the courage of New York's police officers as well as to the selfless sacrifices of untold numbers of civilians. Yet, amid countless stories still unfolding, it is the heroism of the New York City Fire Department that has become the living heart of the symbol of Ground Zero. From the staggering loss of 343 men to their unflagging efforts to "bring their brothers home," New York's firefighters have both portrayed and evoked what is noblest in the American and human spirit. While these firefighters are honoring the deep tradition of their department, their dedication reflects the universal passion of the workers at Ground Zero and the families of victims not yet identified. The digging and excavation, the cranes and trucks that gave this holy ground the look of a construction site are all guided by the overarching priority of recovering human remains. From the beginning, every aspect of the cleanup effort has been engineered to facilitate this recovery.

Focus for a moment on these somber frames of what would become ritual practice: Debris lifted by cranes from the mountain of rubble is first sifted at the site for visible signs of victims' body parts, clothing, or items of identification, and then loaded onto flatbed trucks. Headed to Staten Island, the slow, lumbering vehicles move away from the site like a procession of funeral pyres. The sobering cargo is deposited at Fresh Kills landfill where a carefully orchestrated and specially outfitted crew of volunteers is dispersed over a moonscape of choking dust. Indeed, the hot, protective suits they are required to wear are astronautlike in appearance. Equipped with tiny rakes, each crewmember combs painstakingly through the few square feet of dust and rubble that is her charge. Occasionally, a crewmember uncovers a ring or a necklace, a scrap of clothing, or the contents of a wallet. But sometimes she uncovers a piece of human flesh, a fragment of a body part, a recognizable finger or bit of scalp. Her visceral reaction, a disorienting and debilitating mingling of horror and grief, is not unexpected. Chaplains move silently among the volunteers, offering to pray with them at just such moments. The atmosphere is heavy with mournful reverence. The reverence testifies to the sacredness of what is sought.

What is sought, painstakingly at this secondary site and at Ground Zero, is human flesh. The passion to recover human flesh is the passion to identify unattached parts by connecting them to whole lives with unique personal histories, to restore these physical fragments to the relationship which defined them as individuals, to facilitate the healing process in families still aching for closure of gaping, open wounds.

The passion to recover the flesh of the victims at Ground Zero has been articulated in terms of the desire for closure, the desire to give as many families, as many communities as possible the opportunity to provide a loved one with proper burial. The sacredness of the flesh sought here has been portrayed time and again in the honor guard flanking every corpse carried out of the rubble, in the flags draped, the prayers uttered, the silences observed. Now it is time to articulate in larger terms just what this passion for saving flesh at Ground Zero symbolizes for the world.

ARTICULATING INCARNATION

Theological reflection on the symbol of Ground Zero from a Christian standpoint evokes the reality of the Incarnation. At the heart of the Christian Mystery is the belief that God became flesh in the person of Jesus Christ. God, the Eternal One, Wisdom of the universe's unfolding, Initiator of an age-old covenant with human beings, entered history in the concrete particularity of one Jesus of Nazareth. The particular life of this first-century Jew became the definitive vehicle of the covenant, the vessel and arbiter of the divine/human reconciliation. The flesh of Jesus of Nazareth became, for Christians, the very substance of God's relationship with the world for all eternity. What the particularity of Jesus' life reveals about the nature of destiny of all human flesh is inseparable from the revelation of God in Christ.

The symbol of Ground Zero may be illuminated by reflection on the characteristics of the particular, concrete humanity of Jesus. Born in humble circumstances and raised in a pious Jewish household, Jesus was steeped in the promises of the God of Israel. His intimacy with the God of his ancestors became the ground of his life, his teaching, and his ministry to all whose humanity was in any way diminished. In the power of his words and the inclusivity of his relationships Jesus revealed a God who sides with the poor, chooses the vulnerable, and embraces the stranger. Those who were oppressed encountered in Jesus the Truth that engenders freedom, and they began to live in the power of that Truth. That meant, in concrete terms, the breakdown of accepted hierarchies of power in spheres both secular and religious. Wherever this occurred, the reign of God became visible, and the reign of human authority, religious and secular, mounted an angry defense. Jesus revealed God's will for humanity in his solidarity with the most vulnerable even when it became clear that this would cost him his life. The structures of power, then as now, were threatened by Truth in the flesh. The mighty appeared victorious in putting to death on a cross the one whose life was an affront to their security. But God raised that one up, vindicating the message of his life and ministry. God raised him up, and with him, the future of all those whose cause he championed. The flesh of Jesus raised to new life points to the victory of the sacred inherent in all human flesh, however persecuted, victimized, or fragmented. Christian faith in the life, death, and resurrection of Jesus signals a new valuation of the human condition and freedom from all worldly standards of power. Those who exalt the divinity of the flesh of Jesus exalt the poor, the suffering, and the powerless victims of this world. Those who put faith in the defenseless God of Jesus stand in solidarity with the vulnerable of this world, issuing a challenge to all who would wield power with violence.

This is the truth of Christian faith; without doubt, many still oppose it, wiggle away from it, or seek to temper its critical force. Authentic following of Jesus is an uncomfortable and unpopular affair. Because we are all sinners, none of us who claims to be Christians lives this truth perfectly. Humbly acknowledging as much, we are yet bound to proclaim it and hold it as our standard. It is, after all, the standard of Christ. The United States is a nation which, for all of its diversity, considers itself generically Christian. Indeed, throughout the world, our country is perceived to be "a Christian nation." It is beyond the scope of this chapter to analyze the evident dichotomies in such an identification. The United States of America is the world's greatest economic and military power, and it is well understood that the attacks on the World Trade Center and the Pentagon were attacks on the symbols of that power. Moreover, the attacks constituted a response to the oppressive manner in which the United States has wielded that power among the vulnerable and voiceless nations of the world. This in no way mitigates the horror of what occurred on September 11. It is, however, the sobering reality of our national persona in the world. As Americans we are challenged to gaze at our true face among the nations; we are challenged to peer unflinchingly into those particular features whose arrogance has grown familiar to people at the bottom of the global hierarchy of power and wealth. If we fail to meet this challenge, we desecrate the memory of the victims and the heroes of September 11; we render their sacrifice vain in the valuation of the future. The future really is in our hands. Indeed, we stand now on that fragile edge of the future where hope itself has conditions.

HOPE AT GROUND ZERO

The conditions of a future, the conditions of our hope—indeed, the living presence of that hope—abide in the symbol of Ground Zero. The passion for saving human flesh that has marked this site harbors the seeds of our salvation. On this ground, Americans of all stripes have experienced together the dramatic contrasts of life's extremes. Experiences of victimization and of heroism, of inadequacy and mastery, of isolation and solidarity, experiences of vulnerability and of strength: these belong to all of us. Our ownership of these experiences, with all the implications of their inherent contrast, will provide us with the conditions of our hope, the conditions of our future.

Saving flesh at Ground Zero reveals that in laying hold of our vulnerability we lay hold of our strength. Reverence for human remains, heroic efforts to recover the lost, even the dread some workers feel as they face the day when they can no longer labor at the site, no longer keep vigil in the presence of victims, all of this testifies to the hope that claims a future. The future can only be ours, though, when we recognize that it belongs equally to everyone. The fragility of flesh known in the painful particularities of Ground Zero summons us to submit to its authority as a universal symbol. Only in its universality does it have power to save; only thus does it become the symbol the world cries out for, the symbol by which to gauge what is true and trustworthy amid the disintegration of worldly (and religious) structures of authority.

The captivating force of the image of Ground Zero lies in the myriad manifestations of authentic human *being* evoked by conditions of shared human vulnerability. During the crisis of September 11 human beings instinctively risked taking responsibility for the voiceless victims remaining in the Pit. The future depends now upon our willingness to take responsibility for voiceless victims around the world. The vulnerability we have known is transformed into strength when we let it lead us into solidarity with the most vulnerable people of our world. The bonds forged among Americans in crisis must not end at our shores. The reverence shown for the victimized flesh of fellow citizens must extend to all human victims of violence, oppression, and economic injustice. Such reverence entails humility, and humility is what we will need to face the truth about our responsibility for the victimization of others. We participate in that victimization as individuals and as a nation when we fail to perceive how our choices, our values, our very standard of living as Americans impact the lives of others around the world. We participate in that victimization when we close our eyes to the ways in which the global economy that benefits our society rides roughshod over developing nations, enriching the comfortable and further impoverishing the poor. We participate in the victimization when we fail to widen the horizons of our personal and communal vision and when we fail to call our leaders to accountability according to a global vision not based on American security, power, and privilege. By contrast, we liberate victims, give voice to the voiceless, and achieve our own transformation when our relationship with the vulnerable of our world becomes the arbiter of our choosing.

CONCLUSION: THE FUTURE IN LIFE FOR THE WORLD

No, it is not too much to say that in this historical moment, the future is in our hands. Our hope may be in God, but the God of Jesus Christ entrusts the future of the world to us. The authority we seek in negotiating that future may be available to us in the symbol of Ground Zero, a concrete symbol of the transforming power of our relationship to fragile, human flesh. Firefighters, police officers, ironworkers, and volunteers at Ground Zero ask, as work at the site nears an end, "What do we do now?" It is the question we all must ask ourselves. What do we do now? We seek the source of the symbol's power. We take what has been revealed on this particular ground and live into its universal implications. The efficacy of community. The substance of daily presence transformed into life for others. Life for the world?

In some way, the human acts of courage and the extraordinary sacrifices revealed in stories still unfolding have become life for the world. Lives given selflessly, flesh and blood sacrificed, saving bonds forged among strangers. It all contributes to the light that outshines the darkness, salvation from sin and evil, and the assurances that God will have the last word. By this flesh we are saved.

XIII

JOKING WITH GOD IN A FRAGILE WORLD

WENDY DONIGER

SEPTEMBER 11: WHEN IS IT OK TO JOKE?

The September 16, 2001, issue of the Sunday *New York Times* bore on its front page this notice: "Several of today's sections, including The Times Magazine and The Sophisticated Traveler, went to press before the terrorist attacks last week. The Times regrets that some references to events are outdated, and that the tone of some articles and advertising is inconsistent with the gravity of the news." For weeks after that, professional comedians agonized over when it was safe to joke, and about what sorts of jokes were permissible and which were not. Articles started appearing in the *New York Times* entitled "Comedy Returns, Treading Lightly" [September 26] and "Live from New York, Permission to Laugh" [October 1]. The *Onion*, a weekly newspaper that was based in Chicago but had, in an irony of history, just moved to New York in July of 2001, was one of the first publications to joke successfully about September 11, in its September 27 edition. That issue joyously welcomed by its readers, who carried the paper around with them for days as a kind of security blanket that somehow reassured them that life was still possible, still good, that things were beginning to be normal again.

One article remarked that Jay Leno "started telling Osama bin Laden jokes, based on the 'Springtime for Hitler' model that says it's OK to make fun of the bad guy."[1] This is of course a far older "model" than "Springtime for

Hitler." Such films began even before the official opening of World War II, with a now-forgotten Three Stooges film that mocked Hitler in 1938. Then came Charlie Chaplin's *The Great Dictator* [1940] and Ernst Lubitsch's *To Be or Not To Be* [1942], starring Jack Benny and Carole Lombard, and Carl Reiner's *The Producers* [1968]. But these films carefully avoided the subject of the Holocaust. Films joking about the Holocaust came later, with Agnieszka Holland's *Europa, Europa* [1991], about a Jewish boy who passed for a non-Jew and had to devise ways to conceal the fact that he was circumcised, and, more recently, Roberto Benigni's *Life Is Beautiful* [1998], about an Italian Jew who was taken, with his wife and their four-year-old son, to a concentration camp where he died, though his wife and son survived; he saved his son by pretending that they were playing a game. All of these films were accused of being in bad taste, and *Life Is Beautiful* came under particularly heavy fire from Richard Schickel's *Time* magazine review entitled, "Fascist Fable: A Farce Trivializes the Horror of the Holocaust."[2] The author accuses the film of trying to "travesty tragedy," and he concludes: "The witnesses to the Holocaust—its living victims—inevitably grow fewer every year. The voices that would deny it ever took place remain strident. . . . In this climate, turning even a small corner of this century's central horror into feel-good popular entertainment is abhorrent. Sentimentality is a kind of fascism too, robbing us of judgment and moral acuity, and it needs to be resisted. *Life is Beautiful* is a good place to start." This is a strong indictment indeed, yet many thoughtful people found the film quite wonderful, and it won three Academy Awards. The *Time* magazine reviewer implies that this film denies the reality of the Holocaust by depicting a man who pretends to his son that it is a game. But the film is quite the opposite; it says, there was a Holocaust, and one child who was caught in it survived by pretending that he thought it was a game. I want to argue here that the sort of bitter humor that characterizes *Life Is Beautiful* is precisely what we need to come to terms with in our own reactions to the events of September 11, 2001, and that it is even more effective when it is framed by a theological imagination that includes God in the joke.

THE USES OF GALLOWS HUMOR

We may make terror tolerable by looking it in the eye and joking about it. By joking we reframe the episode in our own terms, transforming it from a passive suffering thrust upon us into an active response to the world; we take possession of it by retelling it in terms that the perpetrator could not. The philosopher Ted Cohen writes that "joking is almost always out of place when it is a kind of avoidance; a laugh should not be a deflection from something else that needs to be done."[3] Black humor is designed precisely to uncover the naked truth, however painful that flaying may be. Terry Southern reported a conversation he had with Stanley Kubrick about *Dr. Strangelove*, in which Kubrick told him that he was going to make a film about "our failure to understand the dangers of nuclear war." He said that he had thought of the story as a "straightforward melodrama" until one morning when he "woke up and realized that nuclear war was too outrageous, too fantastic, to be treated in any conventional manner." He said he could only see it now as "some kind of hideous joke."[4]

What the Germans call *Galgenhumor* is a word that only later enters English from the German in translation, as gallows humor.[5] Given the course of human history, it should not be surprising to find that it is a Jewish specialty.

Let me give you an example of a Jewish gallows joke that is literally about a gallows:

> As World War II drew toward a close, the advancing Russians came upon a town only recently vacated by the retreating Germans. They went to the Jewish ghetto and found that every single Jew—man, woman, and child—had been hung from hastily erected gallows. As they stared in silence, one Russian soldier said to another, "Look what a horrible thing those barbaric Germans have done; they have hung every single Jew in the town." "Yes," said the other, "it is a terrible thing. They didn't leave a single one for us to hang."

This is humor as raw as it gets; one has to have a very low opinion of the human race to find comfort in such a story. And yet it is well known among Jews. A milder version of gallows humor occurs in *Life Is Beautiful*, when Joshua sees a sign in a store that says, "No Jews or dogs allowed," and asks Guido about it. "Yes," says Guido, "everyone does that, some say no Spaniards or horses; let us have a sign in our store, too: no spiders or Visigoths." In *To Be or Not To Be*, when the actor playing Hitler enters, salutes, and says, "Heil myself!" the director says, "No, I don't want a laugh here," but one of the Jewish actors says, "A laugh is nothing to sneeze at." When I spoke about this topic in Leiden, in December of 2001, one of my Dutch colleagues suggested as a title, "The Shoa Must Go On."[6] In real life, too, gallows humor is always an option. Otto Klemperer's wife used to tell this story about her own experience when she had reached California after a narrow escape from the Holocaust: She went out to buy oranges, and the fruit seller asked her, "For juice?" and she said, "Oh my god, here too?"[7]

Now may well be a good season for gallows humor. In Michael Ondaatje's novel about the genocide in Sri Lanka, *Anil's Ghost*, the people who work in the morgue with the corpses of victims of terrorist attacks engage in what Ondaatje calls "a principle of necessary levity": they name their bowling team the "Fuck Yoric School of Forensics," and one of them says, "You've got to have a sense of humor about all this. Otherwise it makes no sense." But Ondaatje's narrator comments: "You must be in hell if you can seriously say things like that."[8] Since a lot of people are in hell a lot of the time, a sense of humor often comes in handy.

THE MICROSCOPIC AND TELESCOPIC VIEWS OF TRAGEDY AND COMEDY

For days after September 11, nothing was the same. But gradually, and not without feelings of guilt, we began, not to forget, but to bracket our shock and grief and sorrow and get on with our lives. We turned away from the figures of death and began to be caught up in the precious trivia of our family and professional life. Some benighted soul bracketed his grief so completely as to create a computer virus that masqueraded as one of the many appeals to peace protests that appeared on our e-mails. Such grotesque cynicism jarred us back into our original shocked concern and again mocked us for caring about buying books while so many of our fellow Americans could do nothing but hope to be able to bury their dead. We suffered from a mild version of survivors' guilt.

It was difficult for us simultaneously to go on living with concern for the longer lines at the airport and the rising costs of fuel and at the same time to stay fully aware of the bodies still lying under that rubble. We strove to keep both of these levels of vision alive in us at the same time. But how? Good films about war teach us how to balance the microscopic view of our daily lives against the telescopic view of cosmic disaster.[9] The telescopic view, which activates our self-irony, and the microscopic view, which activates our sympathy, share at least one essential feature: both are self-distancing.[10] Both self-irony and sympathy pluck us out of our immediate preoccupation with ourselves and our own woes, though in different directions: self-irony allows us to see ourselves through a telescope, while sympathy allows us to see other people no longer through a telescope but through a microscope.

At the end of *All Quiet on the Western Front* (1930),[11] a classic film about World War I, though made with one eye on the early stirrings of World War II, we hear a shot, our hero falls, and we see, against the background of a field of white crosses, a line of soldiers marching away, each turning and staring into the camera for a moment, accusingly, before turning back and fading into the field of graves. Forty years later, another film about World War I, *Oh! What a Lovely War* (1969),[12] ends with a kind of quotation of that scene at the end of *All Quiet on the Western Front*. In the later film, the hero whom we have come to know and care about is fighting in the trenches. He is shot, the movie shifts into slow motion and silence, and we see him sitting on the grass at a picnic on a hill in England with his family, full of the mellow drowsiness of sunshine and wine. He leans back against a tree to take a nap, but the tree becomes a white cross that marks his grave, and he vanishes. As the camera zooms back farther and farther from the cross, enlarging our field of vision, we see that the cross on the grave of the soldier we know is just one cross among the millions of crosses marking the graves on the battlefields of France, one small white tree in a great forest of death. For a second, or perhaps ten seconds, we are able to experience, simultaneously, the intensity of personal grief that we feel for that one soldier and our more general, cosmic sorrow for the astronomical numbers of young men who, as we have long known and long ceased to notice, died in World War I.

This double vision can be achieved in real life, too. On the wall of the central room in the house in Amsterdam where Anne Frank and her family hid from the Nazis, two charts are preserved, side by side. One chart is a column of short, parallel, horizontal lines by which Otto Frank marked the growth of his children over the years, as my father used to mark mine, and I marked my son's. The other chart is a map of Europe with pins marking the advance of the Allied forces—too late, as we now know, to allow that first chart to grow more than a few poignant inches. They are roughly the same size, those two charts, and they represent the tragic intersection of the tiniest, most banal personal concern and a cataclysmic world event.

That precious, banal half of the chart is also the place where the sense of humor is lodged. There is even a gallows joke about the Broadway play based on Anne Frank's diaries, a joke that makes it just over the borderline of acceptable taste precisely because it is *not* about the real Anne Frank, but about the actress who played the part of Anne in the original Broadway production. Susan Strasberg played the part, and played it very badly, by most reports, which I can confirm, having seen her do it; on one occasion, at the end of the play, when the Gestapo came into the building where Anne and her family were hiding, someone in the audience shouted, "She's in the attic." Getting to a place where we can make, or appreciate, that joke means that we have overcome our initial disbelief and have begun to forge ways of living with the reality.

Robert Siegel, the editor of the *Onion*, rightly argued that the act of laughter does not negate the act of crying—"The two are not mutually exclusive."[13] And their head writer, Todd Hansons, agreed: "We're writing . . . not even humor that would make a person laugh. It's more like the kind of humor that would make a person cry."[14] The anthropologist Clifford Geertz writes of "the twin themes of horror and hilarity" in Indonesia: "Nor are the humorous and the horrible always kept rigidly separated, as in that strange scene in one section of the cycle in which several minor witches (disciples of Rangda) toss the corpse of a stillborn child around to the wild amusement of the audience."[15]

To turn the *Time* magazine critic's words around, we must "travesty tragedy," recalling, by the way, that travesty, tragedy, and comedy are all theatrical terms, predisposing us to think of our extreme emotions as dramatic representations. When the Greeks invented tragedy, they always ended each cycle of three tragedies with a satyr play—a satire. Socrates makes this point in Plato's *Symposium*: "The true poet must be tragic and comic at once, and the whole of human life must be felt as a blend of tragedy and comedy."[16] In an old *New Yorker* cartoon, the stereotyped bourgeois lady in a hat, talking with a man in an antique store, has just asked a question about a pair of masks of comedy and tragedy that she holds in her two hands, the caption to which is his reply: "I'm sorry, madam, we only sell them as a set." We assume that she wants only the comic mask, but many people, including the critics who damned *Life Is Beautiful*, want only the tragic. But if we learn anything from this consideration of black humor it is that even when people know that their jokes may injure sensitive feelings, or bring accusations of bad taste, or even get them fired, still they will do it, so great is our need for humor in times of crisis.

My mother, who was Viennese, told me this joke about German and Viennese attitudes to tragedy, war, and terror:

> Near the end of the war, as the Allies were advancing toward Berlin, the German high command sent a message to their Viennese counterparts: "The situation is serious but not hopeless [*ernst aber nicht hofnungslos*]." The Viennese replied, "Here it is quite the opposite: hopeless but not serious [*hofnungslos aber nicht ernst*]."

Naturally, my mother was on the side of the Viennese, but I think Johan Huizinga was, too, when he wrote that "The play-concept . . . is of a higher order than is seriousness. For seriousness seeks to exclude play, whereas play can very well include seriousness."[17] This dialectic culminated in what I regard as the most significant political statement in *Homo Ludens*: "It is not war that is serious, but peace" [*Nicht der Krieg ist der Ernstfall, sondern der Friede*].[18]

Gallows humor, in films like *Life Is Beautiful*, presents us with a world that is hopeless but not serious. Such humor is not designed to speak to the enemy, the perpetrators, nor to the people who deny the Holocaust; perhaps they will use our humor for evil means, to aid their denial, to say that it was all an illusion. Perhaps such humor cannot reach them at all. We must devise other means to deal with them, and that is another story. Nor can such humor speak to people whose tragic experience simply overwhelms any question of humor; we must respect their sadness. But our gallows humor is the way that we speak to one another, to those among the victims who must survive despite the deniers and for whom humor may be a vital restorative. Robert Siegel was on the mark when he said, "People employ irony and sarcasm—we do—because we're bothered by false sentiment. . . . Part of the healing process is to embrace the petty and insignificant."[19] Roger Rosenblatt remarked that suddenly we no longer lived in an age of irony, an age in which "even the most serious things were not to be taken seriously."[20] But Josh Wolk in *Entertainment Weekly* argued, "No, irony isn't dead, despite its recent obituaries, but what is comedy's place in a serious world?"[21] Central, is my answer.

After September 11, many people whose initial, quite understandable disinclination was never to get into an airplane again, overcame that nervousness by saying, to themselves and others, "If we stop flying, they win." This formulaic statement became so common that Chicago's Second City comedy troupe developed a sketch in which a "clay arts" teacher insists to his depressed class, "If we don't glaze our pottery today, *they win*,"[22] while the producers of Fox's MADtv rejected a stronger version about "sleazy lawyers declaring that they should defy terrorists by living their lives normally and so it was their patriotic duty to sue their mothers."[23] I want to say, if we stop laughing at our own tragedies, they win. But if we can laugh at ourselves in the face of the humorless bullies on both sides of the war, then, as the little boy rightly remarks at the end of *Life Is Beautiful*, "We won." To do this is to say, "Your grim, humorless world is not going to destroy our fragile world of self-mockery. We can still mock ourselves, and you. You are not going to get us. We win." The situation is hopeless but not serious, and, if war is play, peace is all that is serious.

GOD'S BLACK JOKES AND DISASTER FILMS

What sort of a God presides over a world that is not serious? The philosopher Ted Cohen writes that "laughter is an acceptance of the world, like god's laughter."[24] Gallows humor does not exactly laugh with God; rather, it spits in God's eye. The Hasidic view, in particular, jokes about God in dark ways that are made possible in part by a belief that God himself has a sense of humor, is a joker, indeed, rather a rough joker. This darker implication of God's play colors the Book of Job, where God plays a game with Satan at Job's expense. At the end of the story of Abraham and Isaac, God at the last minute allows Abraham to sacrifice a ram instead of his son; Woody Allen's version of this myth has God answer Abraham's complaints by saying, "I jokingly suggest thou sacrifice Isaac and thou immediately runs out to do it." And when Abraham protests, "I never know when you're kidding," God replies, "No sense of humor."[25] Or, as Stephen Mitchell argued of the Book of Job, "God's humor here is rich and subtle."

But in Hindu theology, particularly in the mythology of the god Siva, God's laughter is depicted as full of light, a kind of white wave that bursts out of him and creates worlds for us to play in. To laugh with God is therefore to create, to shine the light of joy out into a world darkened by terror. Hindu philosophy speaks of *lila,* "play," the idea that the whole universe is merely God's sport.[26] Indeed, where Einstein reassured us that God does not play dice with the universe, Hindu theology tells us not only that He (Siva) most specifically *does* play dice, but that He cheats, and is caught cheating (by his wife, Parvati).[27] "God's sport" or *lila* also has another sense that is highly relevant here: it is the belief that the whole world is nothing but a kind of spectacle that God puts on for his own amusement, a play in which it is essential for each of us to determine what role is ours, and to play it.[28]

Some religions—including aspects of Judaism and Hinduism—regard the telescopic view, in which nothing is serious, as the God's eye view, the view of God as auteur (and audience) of our black comedy. This idea is not explicitly expressed in Christian or Jewish theology as frequently as it is in Hinduism, but it is often implicit. More often it is merely said, as Shakespeare put it: "All the world's a stage, And all the men and women merely players,"[29] without naming the playwright. The poet William Butler Yeats said it best, as usual, in "Lapis Lazuli": "Gaiety transfiguring all that dread."

It is in this spirit, I think, that we should approach the disturbing fact that Americans tended to view the terrorist attacks on September 11 as a disaster movie, a phenomenon that also seems to reflect a deep human need to transform terror into art. Anthony Lane entitled his piece for the special issue of the *New Yorker* devoted to the attacks, This Is Not a Movie," and remarked: "It was the television commentators as well as those on the ground who resorted to a phrase book culled from the cinema: 'It was like a movie.' 'It was like "Independence Day."' 'It was like "Die Hard."' 'No, "Die Hard 2."' "Armageddon."' . . . What happened on September 11th was that imaginations that had been schooled in the comedy of apocalypse were forced to reconsider the same evidence as tragic. It was hard to make the switch." This is a reversal of the dictum of Marx's "The 18th Brumaire," that when history is replayed, the second time is comedy. Lane offers an explanation for this reaction: unlike Europeans, Americans have no real experience of such attacks against which to measure this new event: "When a European surveys the wreckage of the towers, he or she will summon, consciously or otherwise, a folk memory of catastrophe. Not 'It's like "Die Hard"' but 'It's like the Blitz,' or 'It reminds me of Dresden.'"[30] Before September 11, Americans were like God, spectators at the extravaganza. The *Onion* depicted Americans as resenting the fact that the movie they were watching was not properly scripted, just as Merlina Mercouri in the film *Never on Sunday* rewrote the ends of the Greek tragedies so that everyone lived happily ever after and went to the seashore. The article in the *Onion*, entitled, "American Life Turns into Bad Jerry Bruckheimer Movie," had a photograph of the Trade Tower wreckage with the caption, "An actual scene from real life," and it quoted people as complaining, "This doesn't have any scenes where Bruce Willis saves the planet and quips a one-liner as he blows the bad guy up" or "This isn't supposed to happen in real life. This is supposed to be something that happens in the heads of guys in L. A. sitting around a table, trying to figure out where to add a love interest" or "If the world were going to suddenly turn into a movie without warning, I wish it would have been one of those boring, talky Merchant-Ivory ones instead."

The reclassification of the attacks as a film continued to color perceptions of real life; according to *Newsweek*, two American women from Waco, Texas, captured by the Taliban and held hostage for five weeks, "often felt as though they were trapped inside a terrifying special-effects action movie," and when they were rescued by U.S. military forces, the father of one of the women said, "I don't think Hollywood could have done it better."[31] When a plane hit a skyscraper in Milan, on April 18, 2002, Francesca Giorgetta, thirty-three, a freelance journalist, told a *New York Times* reporter, "Immediately I thought it was a terror attack. I turned and began running. I had a feeling it was like a movie, like what happened to you in New York."[32] The *Onion* article concludes: "Shocked and speechless, we are all still waiting for the end credits to roll. They aren't going to."[33]

There are further ironies in this American tendency to view violence as film. Some people speculated that it was Osama bin Laden's explicit intention that the attacks should be very filmable, photogenic, a true photo-op, that the pilots chose a nice day with good weather and designed the event to be filmed: the first plane was to attract the cameras, which would then have a perfect shot at the second plane.

September 11 was indeed strangely perfect weather. And, later, Americans viewing the tapes of bin Laden speaking after the attacks insisted that it wasn't true, that the tape had been faked by American technology, that bin Laden hadn't said those things. Here we may hear uncomfortable echoes of the denials of the Holocaust. Once something is like a film, anything is like a film. A side effect noted by both Anthony Lane and the *Onion* was the feeling that disaster films would no longer be acceptable, that the experience of art as "as if" had somehow been spoiled, that the disaster film as a genre had become real and therefore no longer viable as "mere" art, no longer amusing. It was as if the genre had lost its sense of humor. I would draw a different sort of line between life and art here, insisting on a distinction between temporary crisis management and long-lasting ways of making sense of a tragic universe. I think that at the time of crisis, in the midst of our pain, we use the "it's just a dream/play" motif to keep from falling apart with shock and grief, while in the long run we need humor to help us go on living.

Indian philosophy urges us to awaken from the nightmare of our lives—or, indeed, from the pleasant artistic fictions of *lila*—to the true awareness of—of what? This is much debated: God, or godhead, or *moksha*, or *nirvana*. Europeans and Americans do not find this a helpful line to follow under normal circumstances, but we may resort to it in emergencies—and Indian philosophy regards all of life as such an emergency; the Buddha preached that we were all in a house on fire and needed to get out *fast*. Someone suggested that on September 11 Americans awakened from the greedy dreams of the 1990s, when "everybody" got rich quick—except, of course, the poor.

People who have been the victims of violence, such as rape, often dissociate themselves from the scene of the crime by telling themselves that they were not there, that some illusory double experienced the event.[34] It is highly relevant to our concerns here that those who perpetrate violence, too, may seek refuge by absenting themselves from reality in this way; we know this from Robert Louis Stevenson's *Dr. Jekyll and Mr. Hyde* as well as from the insanity defense often invoked in present-day legal actions.[35] More specifically, Robert Jay Lifton's *The Nazi Doctors* documents the ways in which those who perpetrated the atrocities bracketed their moral selves in order to project the responsibility from their evil away from themselves, doing this not merely in order to face others, such as the prosecutors at Nuremberg, but unconsciously, for themselves, in order to be able to face themselves.[36] Such bracketing is also a temporary means by which we, too, can think about unthinkable crises. As Geoffrey O'Brien writes of Alfred Hitchcock, "That the global crisis foreshadowed in *The Lady Vanishes* [1938] and *The Foreign Correspondent* [1940] was real enough had not prevented him from weaving it into graceful, often comic fantasies that established *a quite separate and extremely pleasurable alternate reality.* . . . There was a strange comfort in feeling close, for a while, to that nether realm where we store our shadows, as if for future use."[37] And those shadows, indeed that "extremely pleasurable alternate reality"—for some, films, for others, God—do come in handy in the future, which is now.

NOTES

1. Caryn James, "Live from New York, Permission to Laugh." *New York Times*, October 1, 2001, E6.

2. *Time*, November 9, 1998, vol. 152, no. 19, 116–117.

3. Ted Cohen, *Jokes: Philosophical Thoughts on Joking Matters* (Chicago: University of Chicago Press, 1999), 69.

4. Terry Southern, *Now Dig This: The Unspeakable Writings of Terry Southern* (New York: Grove Press, 2001), 72. I am indebted to Mike O'Flaherty for this passage.

5. The word entered official English quite late. It is not in the 1933 *Oxford English Dictionary* at all, but, in the 2001 on-line version, it is defined as "grim, ironical humor, sick humor." It appears in 1901 in W. D. Howells; in 1935, one citation refers to "what the Germans call gallows-humor"; in 1958, another speaks of "gallows humor that pervades the play." Galgenhumor is also cited as a word used in English: O. Onions (1912) Mencken (1948), "Not a few of these terms show Galgenhumor" (such as "meat-wagon" referring to an ambulance.). W. H. Auden, in *Dyer's Hand. (1963)*, refers to the gravedigger's scene in *Hamlet* as an instance of Galgenhumor.

6. I am indebted to Folkert Jensma, editor in chief of NRC, Amsterdam, for passing this joke on to me.

7. I am indebted to Carol Warshawsky for this story.

8. Michael Ondaatje, *Anil's Ghost* (New York: Alfred Knopf, 2000), 147 and 186.

9. Wendy Doniger, *The Implied Spider: Politics and Theology in Myth* (New York: Columbia University Press, 1997), chap. 1.

10. I am indebted for this insight to Lorraine Daston, personal communication, November 22, 2001.

11. *All Quiet on the Western Front* (1930), written by Lewis Milestone, Maxell Anderson, et al., from the novel by Erich Maria Remarque; directed by Lewis Milestone.

12. *Oh! What a Lovely War* (1969), written by Len Deighton, from the stage show by Joan Littlewood; directed by Richard Attenborough.

13. "Fast Chat the Onion," *Newsweek*, October 15, 2001, 9.

14. Cited by Steve Johnson, "Comedy, Late-Night TV, Back on Scene." *Chicago Tribune*, September 19, 2001, Tempo, 1.

15. Clifford Geertz, "Religion as Cultural System," in *The Interpretation of Cultures* (New York: Basic Books, 1973), 115.

16. Plato, *Symposium,* 223D; cf. *Philebus* 50 B.

17. Johan Huizinga, *Homo Ludens: A Study of the Play Element in Culture* (Boston: Beacon Press, 1938/1955), 45.

18. Huizinga, *Homo Ludens*, 209–211 (in the German edition), 240–42 (in the English edition). This is Huizinga's response to Carl Schmidt. *Homo Ludens. Versuch einer Bestimmung des Spielelementes der Kultur* (Amsterdam: Akademische Verlagsanstalt, Pantheon Verlag, 1939). Second German edition: Basel, Brussels, Cologne, Vienna: Akademische Verlagsanstalt, Pantheon Verlag fuer Geschichte und Politik, 1944. "Printed in Germany" [thus, in English, on ISBN page].

19. "Fast Chat the Onion," *Newsweek*, October 15, 2001, 9.

20. Roger Rosenblatt, in *Time* magazine, cited by Johanna Neuman, "Hear the One about the Traveling Taliban? Three Months after September 11, Humor Is Back," *Chicago Tribune*, December 20, 2001, Tempo, 13.

21. Josh Wolk, "Comic Relief," 12–13.

22. Mark Caro, "Tragedy + Time =," *Chicago Tribune*, November 15, sect. 5, 8.

23. Bryan Tucker, cited by Josh Wolk, "Comic Relief," 12–13.

24. Ted Cohen, *Jokes: Philosophical Thoughts on Joking Matters* (Chicago: University of Chicago Press, 1999), 60.

25. Woody Allen, "The Scrolls," in *Without Feathers,* originally published in *The New Republic* (New York: Warner Books, 1976), 24–28, 27.

26. Wendy Doniger O'Flaherty, *Dreams, Illusion, and Other Realities* (Chicago: University of Chicago Press, 1984).

27. Wendy Doniger, *The Bedtrick: Tales of Sex and Masquerade* (Chicago: University of Chicago Press, 2000); David Shulman and Don Handelman, *God Inside Out: Siva's Game of Dice* (New York: Oxford University Press, 1997).

28. David Haberman, *Acting as a Means of Salvation* (New York: Oxford University Press, 1988).

29. Shakespeare, *As You Like It*, 2.7.138–9.

30. Anthony Lane, "This Is Not a Movie," the *New Yorker*, September 24, 2001, 79–80.

31. Ron Moreau, "Delivered from Evil," *Newsweek*, November 26, 2001, 52–53.

32. *New York Times*, April 19, A3.

33. The *Onion*, op. cit., 1 and 13.

34. Wendy Doniger, *Splitting the Difference: Gender and Myth in Ancient Greece and India* (Chicago: University of Chicago Press, 1998), 79–87.

35. Doniger, *Splitting the Difference*, 255–259.

36. Robert J. Lifton, *The Nazi Doctors: Medical Killing and the Psychology of Genocide* (New York: Basic Books, 1986); Doniger, *Splitting the Difference*, 257.

37. Geoffrey O' Brien, in the *New York Review of Books*, November 15, 2001, 23. I have added the italics.

NAME INDEX

Kennedy, John F., 92
Kennedy, Robert, 92
King, Martin Luther, Jr., 92
Kipling, Rudyard, 74, 77
Klemperer, Otto, 108
Kotlowitz, Alex, 28

Lane, Anthony, 158
Lederman, Leon, 91
Leno, Jay, 145
Lifton, Robert J., 159
Lombard, Carole, 146
Lubitch, Ernst, 146
Luria, Isaac, 115
Luther, Martin, 60, 74

Malraux, Andre, 14
Mann, Thomas, 17
Margalit, Vishai, 127, 128
Marx, Karl, 156
Matthew, Saint, 61
McAloon, Vince, 40
Mercouri, Merlina, 156
Mitchell, Stephen, 155
Muhammad, 114

Nahman, Rabbi, 89
Niebuhr, Reinhold, 14, 122
Niebuhr, Richard, 14
Nietzsche, Friedrich, 24
Nixon, Richard M., 92

O'Brien, Geoffrey, 159
O'Connor, Flannery, 96
Ondaatje, Michael, 148
Otto, Rudolf, 113

Paley, Grace, 21
Paul VI (Pope), 41
Paul, Saint 9, 70, 81, 114, 120, 125
Peter, Simon, 61

Rahner, Karl, 18
Randall, J. Herman, Jr., 76
Romero, Oscar, 69
Rosenblatt, Roger, 153

Sartre, Jean-Paul, 14, 24
Satan, 16
Schickel, Richard, 146
Siegel, Robert, 151, 153
Sobrino, Jon, 69
Southern, Terry, 147
Strasberg, Susan, 151
Stevenson, Robert L., 159

Tillich, Paul, 14, 18, 24
Tolstoy, Leo, 14

Vanier, Jean, 129
Verdi, G., 15

Wiesel, Elie, 105
Willis, Bruce, 157

Yeats, William B., 156
Yoder, John H., 122

Zwick, Louise, 128, 129
Zwick, Mark, 128, 129
Zeira, Rabbi, 86

ABOUT THE CONTRIBUTORS

KAREN ARMSTRONG is a prolific writer and commentator on religious ideas. She spent seven years as a Roman Catholic nun before embarking on a career in writing, teaching, and television broadcasting. Her many books include *A History of God: The 4000 Year Quest for Judaism, Christianity and Islam* (a *New York Times* bestseller); *Islam: A Short History*, *Jerusalem: One City, Three Faiths*, and *Through the Narrow Gate: A Memoir of Spiritual Discovery*.

FREDERICK BUECHNER, an ordained Presbyterian minister, served as chair of the religion department and school minister at Phillips Exeter Academy. He is the author of numerous novels and books of essays, including *Lion Country* (a National Book Award nominee), *Gordic* (a Pulitzer Prize nominee), *The Return of Ansel Gibbs* (winner of the Richard and Hinda Rosenthal Award), *A Long Day's Dying*, *The Magnificent Defeat*, *The Alphabet of Grace,* and *The Clown in the Belfry*.

WILLIAM SLOANE COFFIN fought in World War II, worked for the CIA, studied theology, and became a minister. He was jailed as a civil rights marcher with Martin Luther King Jr. and has long been a voice for peace and justice in America. He is the author of numerous books, including *A Passion for the Possible*, *Once to Every Man*, and *The Heart Is a Little to the Left*.

WENDY DONIGER is Mircea Eliade Professor of the History of Religions at the University of Chicago. She has been president of the American Academy of Religion, and she is a fellow of the American Academy of Arts and Sciences. Her writings range from translations of Sanscrit poems and Hindu myths to books about evil, karma, dreams, and folklore. Among her books are *The Rig Veda: An Anthology, Splitting the Difference: Gender and Myth in Ancient Greece and India, The Implied Spider*, and *The Bedtrick: Tales of Sex and Masquerade.*

VIRGIL ELIZONDO was named by *Time* magazine as one of the spiritual innovators of our time. He is professor of theology at the University of Notre Dame and the Graduate Theological Union, founder of the Mexican American Cultural Center in San Antonio, and author and editor of many books, including *Galilean Journey, Guadalupe: Mother of the New Creation,* and *Way of The Cross.*

STANLEY HAUERWAS is professor of theological ethics at Duke University and the author of some twenty books, including *A Community of Character, The Peaceable Kingdom*, and *With the Grain of the Universe*, his 2001 Gifford Lectures. Known for his sharp critique of contemporary culture and armchair Christianity, Hauerwas was named *Time* Magazine's Theologian of the Year in 2001.

THEODORE M. HESBURGH, C.S.C., is president emeritus of the University of Notre Dame. Awarded the Medal of Freedom, the nation's highest civilian honor, he served on fifteen presidential commissions dealing with issues such as civil rights, peaceful uses of atomic energy, Third World development, and immigration reform. His book, *God, Country and Notre Dame* was a national best-seller.

JAMES LANGFORD is director emeritus of the University of Notre Dame Press, a member of the Core Course faculty at Notre Dame, and president of There Are Children Here, a camp for inner-city children. He is a consulting editor in Religious Studies for the Rowman and Littlefield Publishing Group. Among his eight books are *Galileo, Science and the Church* and *Happy Are They: Living the Beatitudes in America.*

JEREMY LANGFORD is editor-in-chief of Sheed and Ward, an imprint of Rowman and Littlefield Publishing Group. He is engaged in graduate studies in theology as a Bernardin Scholar at the Catholic Theological Union in Chicago. Author of many articles, he is coeditor of *The Journey to Peace* by Joseph Cardinal Bernardin and author of *God Moments: Why Faith Really Matters to a New Generation.*

KATHLEEN MCMANUS, O.P., is a preacher and spiritual guide as well as assistant professor of theology at the University of Portland. A member of the Dominican order, she has done ministerial work in the South Bronx. The author of *The Meaning of Suffering in the Theology of Edward Schillebeeckx,* she is a North American representative to the ongoing *Encuentro Interamericano de Teologas Dominicanas.*

JÜRGEN MOLTMANN is professor of systematic theology emeritus at the University of Tubingen and the author of numerous books, including *Theology of Hope; Religion, Revolution and the Future; The Crucified God; On Human Dignity; Political Theology and Ethics; The Church in the Power of* *the Spirit; The Future of Creation;* and *God in Creation.* Among his many honors are the Elba Literary Prize and the Gifford Lectureship.

LEROY S. ROUNER is professor of philosophy, religion and philosophical theology and director of the Institute for Philosophy and Religion at Boston University. He is the author of *Within Human Experience: The Philosophy of William Ernest Hocking, The Long Way Home* (a memoir), and *To Be at Home: Christianity, Civil Religion, and Human Community.* He is also general editor of Boston University Studies in Philosophy and Religion.

ELIE WIESEL is Andrew W. Mellon Professor in the Humanities at Boston University. He is the author of more than forty books, including novels, portraits, legends, a cantata, plays, and memoirs. His recent books include *All the Rivers Run to the Sea: Memoirs* and *And the Sea Is Never Full: Memoirs 1969–.* He has been awarded the Congressional Gold Medal of Achievement, the Medal of Liberty Award, and the 1986 Nobel Prize for Peace.